A TASTE OF Jackson Hole

. . . selected recipes from favorite restaurants

by

Christine Goodman

Christine Goodman
P. O. Box 3308
Jackson, Wyoming 83001

Additional copies may be obtained by contacting Christine Goodman. For your convenience, order forms are included in the back of the book.

Cover and Illustrations by
Chuck Johnston

ISBN: 0-9633566-0-7

Printed by
Pioneer of Jackson Hole
Jackson, Wyoming

To Erin

And grateful acknowledgement and thanks to all the chefs and restaurant owners who so kindly took time from their demanding and busy schedules to share some of their favorite recipes with us. Their support and excitement for this project was a great encouragement to me!

An extra big thank you to Vicky Gouloff for her able assistance in putting together the Table of Contents, Recipes by Category, and Index; and for her humor and diligence while undertaking the task of proofreading this book.

I want to especially thank my father, Chuck Johnston, for all his wonderful drawings.

With love and gratitude,

Christine

Restaurant Addresses

Alpenhof
P. O. Box 288
Teton Village, WY 83025
(307) 733-3462

Anthony's Italian Restaurant
P. O. Box 3031
62 South Glenwood
Jackson, WY 83001
(307) 733-3717

The Blue Lion
P. O. Box 1128
160 North Millward
Jackson, WY 83001
(307) 733-3912

Cadillac Grille
P. O. Box 925
55 North Cache
Jackson, WY 83001
(307) 733-3279

Dornan's
P. O. Box 39
Moose, WY 83012
(307) 733-2415

Gouloff's
P. O. Box 458
3600 Teton Village Road
Teton Village, WY 83025
(307) 733-1886

The Granary
P. O. Box 3154
1800 N. Spirit Dance Road
Jackson, WY 83001
(307) 733-8833

Jedediah's Original House of Sourdough
P. O. Box 3857
135 East Broadway
Jackson, WY 83001
(307) 733-5671

Jenny Leigh's
P. O. Box 328
3345 W. McCollister Drive
Teton Village, WY 83025
(307) 733-7102

JJ's Silver Dollar Bar and Grill
P. O. Box 69
50 North Glenwood
Jackson, WY 83001
(307) 733-2190

La Chispa Mexican Cafe
P. O. Box 621
25 North Cache
Jackson, WY 83001
(307) 733-4790

Lame Duck Chinese Restaurant
P. O. Box 3248
680 East Broadway
Jackson, WY 83001
(307) 733-4311

Louie's Steak & Seafood
P. O. Box 824
175 North Center
Jackson, WY 83001
(307) 733-6803

Mangy Moose Restaurant & Saloon
P. O. Box 190
3285 W. McCollister Drive
Teton Village, WY 83025
(307) 733-4913

Nora's Fishcreek Inn
5600 West Highway 22
Wilson, WY 83014
(307) 733-8288

Off Broadway Restaurant
P. O. Box 1226
30 South King
Jackson, WY 83001
(307) 733-9777

Rafferty's
P. O. Box SKI
400 E. Snow King Avenue
Jackson, WY 83001
(307) 733-5200

The Range
P. O. Box 328
3345 W. McCollister Dr.
Teton Village, WY 83025
(307) 733-5481

Stiegler's Restaurant and Bar
The Aspens
Teton Village Road
Jackson, WY 83001
(307) 733-1071

Sweetwater Restaurant
P. O. Box 3271
85 South King
Jackson, WY 83001
(307) 733-3553

Teton Pines Restaurant
3450 N. Clubhouse Drive
Jackson, WY 83001
(307) 733-1005

• • • • • • • • • • • • •

Spice Merchant
P. O. Box 524
Jackson, WY 83001
(307) 733-7811

Table of Contents

Recipes by Menu Category

Appetizers

Soups

Salads

Intermezzos

Entrees

Starch

Vegetable

Breads and Baked Goods

Desserts

Alpenhof

Teton Village
733-3462

Opening its doors in 1965 the Alpenhof Lodge was built by Dietrich and Anneliese Oberreit to duplicate the charming inns of Bavaria and Austria. Since its sale in 1988, the new owners have tried to build on that tradition by refurbishing the lodge with original Bavarian furniture, feather beds, and flowers cascading from boxes adorning the outside of the building during the spring and summer months. The goal is to make the Alpenhof as authentic as a well-traveled guest might fondly remember from his travels in Europe. The tradition of European innkeeping is continued by Mike Gebauer, a native of Austria.

The Alpenhof's four-star restaurant offers a cuisine which is basically continental, with some regional influences, served in an elegant yet informal setting. Famous not only for its tableside service which includes Rack of Lamb, Steak Diane, Caesar Salad and the best Bananas Foster west of New Orleans, the Alpenhof is also known for its extensive variety of game dishes from caribou to elk and red deer.

Starting new in the Winter of 1992, Dietrich's Bar will offer real bistro dining. Already known for its lunches and apres ski, the bar will serve hearty fare at very reasonable prices.

Chef Michael Burke, classically trained in Europe 20 years ago, shares with us several of his own creations to create two deliciously wonderful menus.

MENU FOR SIX

Old English Pate

Dutch Chervil Soup

Scallop Salad
with Cumin Dressing

Pork Medallions Carbonari

Rye Rice Pilaf

Green Beans
with Fresh Chestnuts

Stuffed Tomatoes

English Trifle

Chef Michael Burke

OLDE ENGLISH PATE

Serves 6

In skillet, combine and saute for 10 minutes. . .	3	**tablespoons**	***unsalted butter***
	2	**small**	***onions,*** chopped
	4	**ounces**	***country sausage***
	1	**medium**	***apple,*** peeled and chopped
	1	**tablespoon**	***dried rosemary***
	1 1/2	**teaspoons**	***salt***
	1 1/2	**teaspoons**	***white pepper***
	1 1/2	**teaspoons**	***ground thyme***
	1/2	**teaspoon**	***dried basil***
	1/2	**teaspoon**	***nutmeg***

Add and saute until browned. . .	1 1/4	**pound**	***chicken livers***

Place ina 350° oven for 7 minutes. Remove and Cool.

In food processor, combine the liver mixture and. . .	1 3/4	**cups**	***unsalted butter,*** softened
	1 1/2		***eggs,*** hard cooked
	2	**tablespoons**	***cognac***
	1	**tablespoon**	***dry sherry***
	1	**tablespoon**	***parsley,*** chopped

Puree until smooth.

Firmly pack mixture into a terrine; cover with plastic and chill overnight. To serve, set the terrine in hot water for a moment or two before turning the pate out onto a serving plate. (Another trick which makes unmolding of the pate quite easy is to line the terrine with plastic wrap before filling with the pate mixture.)

An alternate method of preparing this pate, which creates an elegant presentation, is to line the terrine with strips of uncooked bacon, and firmly pack the mixture inside. Cover with more strips of bacon. Place the terrine in a baking pan and pour enough water in the baking pan to come half way up the sides of the terrine. Bake pate in this water bath in a preheated 325° oven for 1 hour. Allow to cool to room temperature before refrigerating overnight. To serve, turn pate out of terrine onto platter.

DUTCH CHERVIL SOUP

Serves 6

In stockpot, over medium heat, combine to make a smooth roux. . .	6	tablespoons	*butter*
	8	tablespoons	*flour*
Stirring constantly, cook for 3 minutes.			
Add, one cup at a time, stirring after each addition. . .	8	cups	*hot beef stock**
Cook for 10 minutes more over medium heat. **Do not allow to boil.**			
Add. . .	5	tablespoons	*fresh chervil,* chopped
Remove from heat.			
In large bowl, whip. . .	6		*egg yolks*

Whisking continuously, slowly add soup to whipped egg yolks. Pour soup back into stockpot, add *salt and pepper to taste,* and heat at a very low flame. **Do not allow soup to boil,** as eggs <u>will</u> curdle. Serve in warmed soup bowls.

**Homemade is best (see recipe, page 259), or use a good quality canned beef consomme.*

SCALLOP SALAD WITH CUMIN DRESSING

Serves 6

In bowl, combine and mix well. . . *(dressing)*	6	**tablespoons**	***olive oil***
	$1^1/_4$	**tablespoons**	***dry sherry***
	2	**tablespoons**	***ground cumin,*** fresh
	1		***jalapeno pepper,*** seeded & finely diced
			salt and pepper to taste
Set aside.			

In saucepan, bring to a boil. . . *(court boullion)*	3	**cups**	***water***
	1	**cup**	***dry white wine***
	1	**tablespoon**	***thyme leaf***
	6	**whole**	***black peppercorns***
	1		***bay leaf***

Add and cook for two minutes. . .	1	**pound**	***bay scallops***
Drain scallops and allow them to cool.			

To complete this recipe, you will need. . .	1	**large**	***tomato,*** peeled, seeded and diced
	4	**whole**	***scallions,*** chopped
	1	**head**	***radicchio,*** shredded

Toss the cooled scallops and dressing with the *diced tomato* and *chopped scallions*. Taste for seasoning and serve on beds of *radicchio.*

PORK MEDALLIONS CARBONARI

Serves 6

Named after Master Chef, Tony Carbonari, whom Michael apprenticed under, this dish won a Silver Medal at the Hotel Olympia Culinary Fare in London in 1976.

Remove fat and silverskin from. . . **2** **pounds** ***pork tenderloin***

Slice tenderloins into 1/4" slices; season with salt and pepper.

In skillet, over medium heat, saute for 1 minute. . .

3	**tablespoons**	***unsalted butter,*** melted
2	**tablespoons**	***fresh shallots,*** chopped
1	**tablespoon**	***fresh garlic,*** minced

Add pork and saute until brown on both sides. Remove pork and keep warm in oven while preparing sauce.

In same skillet, add and saute for 3 minutes. . .

1	**cup**	***mushrooms,*** sliced
1	**cup**	***celery,*** julienne
1/2	**cup**	***green bell pepper,*** julienne
1/2	**cup**	***red bell pepper,*** julienne
1/2	**cup**	***yellow bell pepper,*** julienne

Deglaze skillet and vegetables with. . .	1/2	**cup**	***brandy***
Reduce liquid by half and add. . .	1	**cup**	***demi-glace****
Reduce by one third and add. . .	2	**tablespoons**	***heavy cream***

Reduce sauce to a silky consistency. Serve pork medallions draped with sauce.

**Homemade is best (see recipe on page 259), or a good quality demi-glace can be purchased in some gourmet food stores.*

RYE RICE PILAF

Serves 6

In heavy saucepan, saute until lightly browned. . .	1/2	**cup**	***butter***
	1/4	**cup**	***vermicelli,*** broken
Add and saute until rice is very hot. . .	1	**cup**	***white rice,*** uncooked
	1	**cup**	***rye flakes***
	1/4	**cup**	***onion,*** diced
Reduce heat to low and add. . .	4	**cups**	***water,*** boiling
			salt and pepper to taste

Cover and cook for 20 minutes. Remove lid and continue cooking until all moisture has evaporated. Fluff pilaf with fork and serve immediately.

GREEN BEANS WITH FRESH CHESTNUTS

Serves 6

In a hot skillet combine...	1	**tablespoon**	***vegetable oil***
	$^{3}/_{4}$	**cup**	***chestnuts,*** whole in the shell
Sear chestnuts for 2-3 minutes, then add...	$^{1}/_{4}$	**cup**	***port***

Place skillet in a 325° oven to roast for about 1 hour, until the shells pop. Allow chestnuts to cool, then chop coarsely and set aside.

Steam until tender crisp (about 3-4 minutes)...	2	**pounds**	***fresh green beans,*** trimmed and split lengthwise

---

In skillet, saute for approximately 3 minutes...	3	**tablespoons**	***butter***
	$^{1}/_{2}$	**cup**	***chestnuts,*** chopped
	4		***scallions,*** white part only, minced
Nuts should be aromatic.			

To complete this recipe, you will need...	1	**tablespoon**	***fresh lemon juice***
			black pepper, freshly ground to taste

Add green beans to pan with nuts, toss thoroughly and saute for half a minute to heat through. Sprinkle with *fresh lemon juice* and *black pepper* .

STUFFED TOMATOES

Serves 6

In boiling water, blanch. . .	**6**	**medium**	***tomatoes***
Slice tops of tomatoes off (save tops) and core.			

In skillet, combine and saute for 1 minute. . .	**1/4**	**cup**	***unsalted butter,*** melted
	1	**tablespoon**	***shallots,*** diced
	1/2	**tablespoon**	***fresh garlic,*** minced

Add. . .	**1/4**	**cup**	***dry white wine***
	2	**cups**	***dry duxelle****
	3	**tablespoons**	***parmesan cheese,*** freshly grated
	1	**tablespoon**	***leaf oregano***
	1 1/2	**cups**	***fresh parsley,*** chopped
	2	**tablespoons**	***fresh basil,*** chopped
Cook until liquid is reduced by two thirds.			

Stuff the prepared tomatoes with mixture. Bake uncovered in a **preheated** 325° oven for 10 minutes. Place reserved tomato lids on top and serve.

Dry duxelle is made by combining equal parts **finely chopped onion and **finely chopped mushrooms** and sauteing in a small amount of butter until moisture is released by the mushrooms and then all moisture evaporates.*

ENGLISH TRIFLE

Serves 6

Easy to make and traditionally a great dessert!

For this recipe, you will need...			
	1	**9" round**	***sponge layer cake***
	1/4	**cup**	***raspberry jam***
	3	**tablespoons**	***sherry***
	2	**cups**	***fresh fruit,*** sweetened (or fruit cocktail)
	1/4	**cup**	***almonds,*** blanched and slivered

Spread top of *cake* with *jam* and place in a deep-dish glass bowl. Sprinkle cake with *sherry,* top with the *fruit,* then sprinkle with the *almonds.* Cover and keep cool in the refrigerator while preparing the **Custard**.

Custard

In top of double boiler, over boiling water, mix together...			
	3/4	**cup**	***sugar***
	2	**tablespoons**	***cornstarch***
	1	**pinch**	***salt***

Stirring constantly, slowly add...	**1**	**cup**	***milk***
	1	**cup**	***heavy cream***

Cover and cook for 8 minutes. Uncover and cook 10 minutes longer, stirring occasionally. **Do not allow custard to boil.**

Stirring constantly, add...	**4**		***egg yolks,*** well beaten
	2	**tablespoons**	***butter,*** broken into pieces

Cook for 3 minutes, stirring constantly. Allow to cool, stirring occasionnally.

Stir in...	**1 1/2**	**teaspoons**	***pure vanilla extract***
then fold in...	**1**	**cup**	***heavy cream,*** whipped

Pour finished custard over trifle and let cool in refrigerator. Custard should set up to whipped cream consistency.

MENU FOR SIX

Escargot en Croute
with Pesto and Bechamel Sauce

Mushroom Soup
with Spinach Threads

Duck Breast Helene
with Fresh Pear

Roast Potatoes

Fresh Carrots

Ranch Pudding
with Whiskey Whipped Cream

Chef Michael Burke

ESCARGOT EN CROUTE

Serves 6

A meeting of the minds of Michael and his chefs at the Alpenhof created this masterpiece — a real epicurean delight!

In skillet, saute together. . .

1/4	**cup**	***butter,*** melted
1	**tablespoon**	***shallots,*** minced
1	**tablespoon**	***fresh basil,*** minced
1 1/2	**teaspoons**	***garlic,*** minced
36		***french snails*** (medium size)

Set aside.

In another skillet, saute. . .

2	**tablespoons**	***butter,*** melted
3/4	**cup**	***mushrooms,*** minced
3/4	**cup**	***onions,*** minced

Cook until mushrooms release moisture and until most of the moisture has evaporated —

To complete this recipe, you will need. . .

1/3	**cup**	***melted butter***
12	**sheets**	***phyllo dough***
1	**bunch**	***scallions,*** green part only (blanched)
1	**large**	***tomato,*** seeded and diced

Brush one sheet of *phyllo dough* evenly with *butter* (don't miss any edges!). Place another sheet of phyllo directly on top of the first one and brush it with butter. Using knife or pizza cutter, cut rectangle of phyllo into six square sections. Place 2 teaspoons duxelle and one snail into center of each square. Gather four corners of square together and pinch at the top. Tie pinched top with a blanched *scallion* leaf to hold together. Bake 12 to 15 minutes in a **preheated** 350° oven.

To serve, pour warm **Bechamel Sauce** onto the serving plate; pour **Pesto Sauce** in the middle of Bechamel Sauce and, using a tooth pick, draw it out from the center to create a star shape. Cluster 6 snail en croutes in the middle of the star and garnish with *diced tomato*. Viola!

Bechamel Sauce

In heavy saucepan, combine. . .	**6**	**tablespoons**	***melted butter***
	5	**tablespoons**	***flour***
Cook for 2 minutes without browning flour.			
While stirring, slowly add. . .	**2 1/2**	**cups**	***half and half***
Season with. . .	**1**	**pinch**	***ground white pepper***
	1	**pinch**	***nutmeg***

Cook, stirring occasionally, until sauce is consistency of very thick cream. Keep warm or refrigerate if made ahead of time. If sauce is refrigerated, bring it to temperature slowly in a heavy saucepan over low heat, stirring occasionally.

Pesto Sauce

In food processor, puree. . .	**2**	**cups**	***fresh basil,*** firmly packed
	3/4	**cup**	***parmesan cheese***
	1/4	**cup**	***pine nuts*** (or walnuts)
	4	**cloves**	***garlic***
With processor still running, slowly add. . .	**1/2**	**cup**	***olive oil***

Pesto sauce should be the consistency of heavy cream. Check consistency of the pesto sauce before adding the entire half cup of olive oil. Sometimes a little less or a little more than a half cup of olive oil is needed.

MUSHROOM SOUP WITH SPINACH THREADS

Serves 6

In a heavy saucepan, over low heat, combine...	3	**tablespoons**	***butter,*** melted
	2	**medium**	***onions,*** chopped
	2	**small**	***garlic cloves,*** halved
	3		***leeks,*** white part only, sliced
Cook, covered, for 25 minutes. Stir occasionally.			

Turn heat up to medium and stir in...	2	**pounds**	***mushrooms,*** chopped
	2	**teaspoons**	***fresh summer savory*** (1 teaspoon dried)
	$^{1}/_{4}$	**teaspoon**	***dried oregano***
Cook until mushrooms render liquid. Reduce heat to low and cook 5 minutes, stirring occasionally.			

Add and simmer for 5 minutes...	$^{1}/_{3}$	**cup**	***Amonkillado Sherry***
Add and bring to boil...	9	**cups**	***chicken stock****
	2	**tablespoons**	***tomato paste***
	1		***bay leaf***
Cover and simmer for about 45 minutes.			

To complete this recipe, you will need...	8	**whole**	***spinach leaves,*** julienne
			ground white pepper
			salt

In food processor, puree soup until smooth. Pour into a clean saucepan and bring to a simmer, seasoning with *white pepper* and *salt*. Stir in *julienne of spinach leaves* and serve.

**Homemade is best (see recipe on page 258), or use good quality canned chicken stock.*

DUCK BREAST HELENE

Serves 6

*French pear brandy, available at fine liquor stores, is a must in this recipe. Using an inexpensive domestic pear brandy **will** alter the flavor of this dish!*

Debone. . .	6	**whole**	***duck breasts***
and rub with	1	**tablespoon**	***Poire William****
	3	**teaspoons**	***ground cumin***
	2	**small**	***garlic cloves,*** crushed
Let marinate at room temperature for at least 1 hour.			

In skillet, over medium high heat, toast. . .	2	**teaspoons**	***whole cumin seeds***
Set aside.			

Peel and slice lengthwise. . .	3		***fresh pears***
Lay fans of pear halves in shallow baking dish. Pour over each fan of pear. . .	1/2	**teaspoon**	***Poire William***
Let pears marinate while you cook the duck.			

Preheat saute pan until very hot; place each duck breast skin side down and cook 7-10 minutes (until golden brown) without turning. Drain off most of the fat and turn breasts over to cook another 7-10 minutes on other side. Place duck breasts on a serving platter and keep in a warm place for about 10 minutes. This allows them to tenderize. Place pears under medium broiler to cook through. (Watch carefully that they don't scorch or burn.)

In saute pan that ducks were cooked in, combine. . .	**2**	**cups**	***white wine***
	2	**tablespoons**	***Poire William***
	1/2	**cup**	***onion,*** chopped
Reduce gently until about 3/4 cup liquid remains.			

Remove pan from heat and stir or swirl in. . .	**18**	**tablespoons**	***butter,*** cold, cut into small squares

Place each duck breast on plate with fan of pear next to it. Sieve the sauce over each breast and sprinkle cumin seeds over pear and duck.

**French pear brandy, available at fine liquor stores.*

RANCH PUDDING WITH WHISKEY WHIPPED CREAM

Serves 6

"A favorite family recipe of my aunt, who was a pastry chef at the Savoy in London." If you prefer, brandy or rum are good substitutes for the whiskey in this recipe.

Into buttered 9-inch square or round baking dish, sprinkle evenly...	1	cup	***pecans or walnuts,*** toasted and chopped
	1	cup	***raisins***

In bowl, beat together until well blended...	1	cup	***dark brown sugar,*** firmly packed
	3/4	cup	***light corn syrup***
	4		***eggs***
	1/4	cup	***whiskey***
	1/4	cup	***butter,*** melted
	1	teaspoon	***vanilla extract***
	1/2	teaspoon	***salt***
Carefully pour this mixture over the raisins and nuts.			

Arrange decoratively on top...	1/2	cup	***pecan or walnut halves,*** toasted

Bake in **preheated** 400° oven for 10 minutes, then reduce oven temperature to 325° and continue baking for about 20-25 minutes, until light golden brown. Serve warm with **Whiskey Whipped Cream.**

Whiskey Whipped Cream

Combine and whip until soft peaks form...	1	cup	***whipping cream***
	2	tablespoons	***whiskey***
	1	tablespoon	***sugar***

Anthony's

62 South Glenwood
Jackson
733-3717

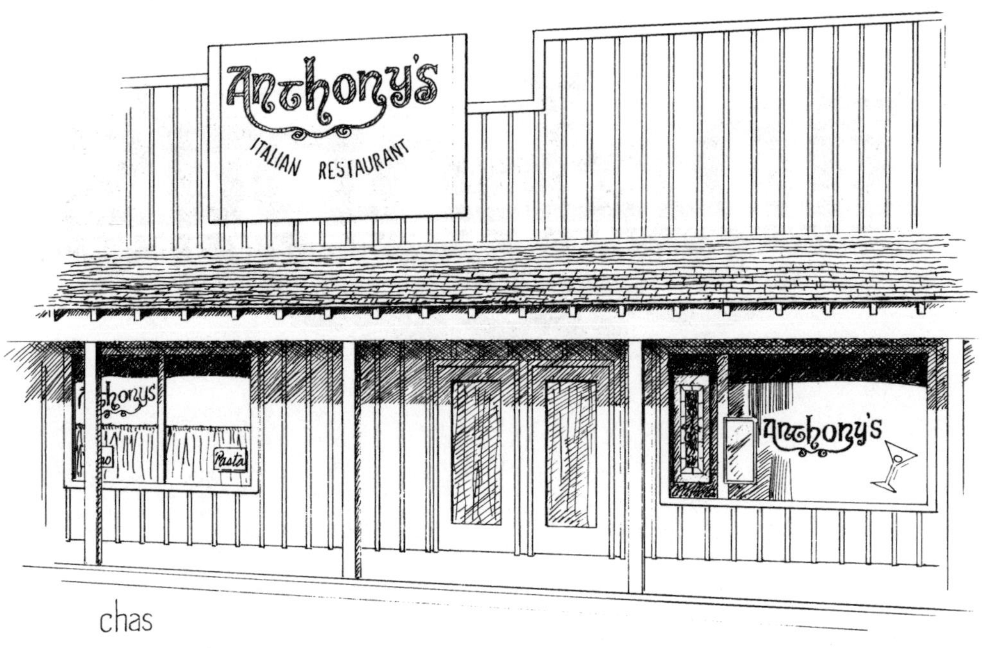

Anthony's Italian Restaurant was opened, at its present location, in February 1977. In September of 1980 Anthony Wall, chef/manager since 1977, assumed ownership of the business. In 1983, Anthony's expanded, taking over the adjacent storefront and adding a full bar and waiting room. Mr. Wall, also an antiques dealer, has decorated the bar with antique beer and liquor advertising, as well as art and memorabilia acquired from various trips to Italy.

Managers Pete Wiswell and Stan Wood and their experienced staff — approximately one half of Anthony's full-time staff has worked there for at least seven years — emphasize consistency and a fun, informal atmosphere which could only be called "Italian style."

All of Anthony's dinners include freshly baked garlic bread, minestrone soup or seafood chowder, salad, entree and dessert, complemented by a full service bar and a wine list which includes an extensive selection of Italian wines. Of course, espresso and cappuccino are available after dinner.

MENU FOR SIX

Fried Eggplant
with Marinara Sauce

Fettuccine al'Antonio

Minestrone

Green Salad with
Anthony's Blue Cheese Dressing

Petti di Pollo al Limon

Spaghettini with Garlic Butter

Spumoni Ice Cream

Chef Anthony Wall

FRIED EGGPLANT WITH MARINARA SAUCE

Serves 6

For this recipe, you will need. . .	**1**	**large**	***eggplant*** (or two small)

Peel, then cut eggplants into 1/4" to 3/8" thick slices. Place slices in a deep pan completely covered with cold water to which a small handful of salt has been added. Store in refrigerator.

In shallow pan, mix together. . .	**1/2**	**cup**	***flour***
	1/2	**cup**	***breadcrumbs***
	1/2	**cup**	***parmesan cheese,*** finely grated
	1	**teaspoon**	***salt***
	1	**teaspoon**	***pepper***
	1	**pinch**	***leaf oregano***
	1	**pinch**	***basil***
	1	**pinch**	***garlic powder***

To complete this recipe, you will need. . .	**2**		***eggs,*** beaten
			vegetable oil

Remove eggplant from the refrigerator, drain off the water and pat dry. Dip each slice completely in *beaten eggs,* then press into breadcrumb mixture. Coat both sides well. Fry in a deep fryer or in a half inch of *vegetable oil,* turning at least once, until golden brown. Serve with **Marinara Sauce.**

Marinara Sauce

In large saucepan, combine. . .	**1/4**	**cup**	***olive oil,*** heated (extra virgin)
	6	**cloves**	***garlic,*** minced
	1	**large**	***yellow onion,*** finely diced

Saute until onions are transparent.

Add to mixture. . .	**1**	**large**	***green bell pepper,*** finely diced
	1	**large**	***red bell pepper,*** finely diced
Saute for 3-4 minutes, stirring constantly to prevent garlic from burning.			
Add and simmer for 3-4 minutes. . .	**1/2**	**cup**	***dry red wine***
Add and simmer over low heat for 45 minutes to an hour. . .	**32**	**ounces**	***canned tomatoes,*** (crushed)
	3	**whole**	***bay leaves***
	1	**teaspoon**	***dried oregano***
	1	**teaspoon**	***dried basil***
	1	**teaspoon**	***salt***
	1	**teaspoon**	***ground black pepper***

If the tomato product used was extremely thick, you may want to add a little water to thin the sauce to the correct consistency. This recipe makes a little over one quart.

FETTUCCINE al'ANTONIO

Serves 6

In boiling water, cook to al dente. . . (still firm in the middle)	$1^1/_2$	**pounds**	***"krinkly" egg noodles***
Drain well.			

In large bowl, mix noodles with. . .	$1^1/_2$	**cups**	***mozzarella cheese,*** shredded
	$1^1/_2$	**cups**	***parmesan or romano cheese,*** freshly shredded (if finely grated, use 1 cup)
	$1^1/_2$	**cups**	***heavy whipping cream***
	1	**teaspoon**	***salt***
	1	**tablespoon**	***black pepper,*** freshly cracked

Place into individual rarebit or casserole pans so that mixture is about 1-1/2 inches thick. Sprinkle with more shredded *mozzarella cheese,* then with more *parmesan cheese.* Bake in a **preheated** 375° oven until golden brown, about 10-15 minutes.

MINESTRONE

Serves 6

In a small stock pot, combine. . .

1/2	**cup**	***olive oil,***
4	**large**	***garlic cloves,*** minced
1	**large**	***carrot,*** diced
1	**medium**	***green pepper,*** diced
1	**medium**	***yellow onion,*** diced
1	**large**	***potato,*** diced
1	**large**	***zucchini,*** cut in half lengthwise and thinly sliced
3	**medium**	***fresh tomatoes,*** diced (with all the juice)

Cook until onions are transparent.

Add to mixture and cook for another 2-3 minutes. . .

1	**large pinch**	***basil***
1	**large pinch**	***leaf oregano***
1	**teaspoon**	***salt***
1	**teaspoon**	***black pepper***
1/2	**cup**	***lentils*** (soaked overnight in water)

Add and bring to a boil. . . **2** **quarts** ***chicken stock****

Remove soup from heat. Salt and pepper again to taste. Serve with freshly grated *parmesan* or *romano cheese.*

**Homemade is best (see recipe page 258), or use good quality canned.*

GREEN SALAD WITH ANTHONY'S BLUE CHEESE DRESSING

Serves 6

Break off leaves and tear by hand, wash and drain...	1	**head**	*iceburg lettuce*
	1	**head**	*red leaf lettuce*

Shred and mix with lettuce in large wooden bowl...	2	**large**	*carrots*
	1/2	**small**	*red cabbage*

Garnish with tomato wedges and croutons. Dress with **Anthony's House Dressing.**

Anthony's Blue Cheese Dressing

Whip together until well blended...	6	**ounces**	*salad oil*
	3	**ounces**	*olive oil*
	4	**ounces**	*apple cider vinegar*
	1	**tablespoon**	*dijon mustard*
	1	**pinch**	*salt*
	4		*garlic cloves,* minced
Fold in...	1/4	**pound**	*blue cheese,* finely crumbled

PETTI di POLLO al LIMON

Serves 6

In large saute pan, heat. . .	**2**	**tablespoons**	***butter***
	2	**tablespoons**	***olive oil***
Add. . .	**4**	**large**	***garlic cloves,*** minced
Immediately add. . .	**6**	**whole**	***chicken breasts,*** skinless and boneless, dredged in flour

Saute until golden brown on both sides. Remove chicken and keep warm.

In same pan, heat an additional. . .	**2**	**tablespoons**	***butter***
	2	**tablespoons**	***olive oil***
Add and cook for 2 minutes, shaking pan often. . .	**2**	**large**	***garlic cloves,*** minced
	2	**large**	***yellow onions,*** thinly sliced
	1	**large head**	***broccoli,*** broken into small florets
Add and cook 2 minutes more. . .	**1/2**	**pound**	***mushrooms,*** thinly sliced

---

Add and cook until liquid is reduced by half. . .	**1 1/2**	**cups**	***dry white wine***
	2		***lemons,*** juice of

Return chicken to pan and add. . .	**3/4**	**cup**	***heavy whipping cream***

Stir or shake and swirl pan to blend sauce together. Cook for 1 minute. Serve the chicken with the vegetables and sauce ladled over the top.

SPAGHETTINI WITH GARLIC BUTTER

Serves 6

In boiling water, cook to al dente. . . (still firm in the center)	**1**	**pound**	*spaghettini noodles*

Rinse with <u>hot</u> water and drain well. Toss with **Garlic Butter.**

If you prefer, top the spaghettini noodles with marinara sauce (recipe on page 24).

Garlic Butter

In saucepan, heat together. . .	**1½**	**tablespoons**	*butter*
	1½	**tablespoons**	*olive oil*
	2	**large**	*garlic cloves,* minced
			salt and pepper to taste

SPUMONI ICE CREAM

Creating your own spumoni ice cream is easy. Simply swirl together equal parts of softened ***cherry vanilla, pistachio,*** and ***chocolate*** ice cream.

160 North Millward
Jackson
733-3912

In the mid-seventies a charming old home was converted to use as the Blue Lion Restaurant, featuring French cuisine. Ned Brown became the proud owner of the Blue Lion in 1978 after spending a summer in Jackson Hole enjoying his love of outdoor sports. Ned had traveled to numerous Rocky Mountain resorts looking for the perfect area to pursue his dream of owning his own restaurant.

Florice Brown, Ned's mother, played an influential part in developing the Blue Lion's cuisine. Some of her recipes for Floridian and Californian style cooking have been used consistently over the past 12 years, including the fudge sauce which adorns one of the locals' favorite desserts — Mud Pie!

Ned and his wife, Sheri, along with their chef, Tim Libassi, have incorporated the French cuisine into a more Continental style menu, stressing the importance of using only the freshest ingredients available. The Blue Lion has its own herb garden on the premises. Fresh fish is flown in daily, and free range veal is featured on the menu. Lighter, full-flavored sauces and salsas accompany most entrees, which include elk, lamb, charbroiled steaks, poultry, seafood, and vegetarian dishes. Home baked breads and desserts are prepared daily. Creative cuisine at its finest!

The Blue Lion has expanded over the years to include a tree shaded patio for summer dining, and an upstairs dining room for private parties and large groups. Truly a locals' favorite for dining out, the Blue Lion also caters so you can enjoy their fine cuisine at home for your special parties!

MENU FOR SIX

Havarti en Croute

Tomato-Feta Salad

Roast Rack of Lamb
with Peppercorn Cream Sauce
and Jalapeno Mint Sauce

Rice Pilaf

Fresh Sauteed Vegetables

Neapolitan Cheesecake

Chef Tim Libassi

HAVARTI EN CROUTE

Serves 6

In skillet, combine and saute for 2 minutes. . .	3	**tablespoons**	***olive oil***
	1/2	**tablespoon**	***garlic,*** minced
	3	**cups**	***mushrooms,*** sliced

Add and cook, covered, for 3 minutes to steam spinach. . .	1/2	**pound**	***spinach,*** chopped (stems removed)
	1/4	**cup**	***white wine***

Remove spinach mixture from heat and let cool in a colander to drain excess liquid.

To complete this recipe, you will need. . .	8	**ounces**	***havarti cheese,*** cut into two slices
	3		***eggs,*** lightly beaten
	1	**sheet**	***frozen puff pastry,*** thawed
			flour

Trim a one-inch strip from one side of the sheet of *puff pastry*. Dust counter surface lightly with *flour*. Roll the pastry sheet into a 15" x 15" square; brush off excess flour. Place half of spinach mixture in center, top with one slice of hav*arti cheese*, then more spinach and finish with the other havarti slice. Brush the puff pastry all around the spinach and havarti with *egg*. Fold one side of the puff pastry sheet over the havarti and brush with egg. Fold the opposite side of the pastry over the top of the first fold of pastry and brush with egg. Follow the same procedure with the remaining sides of pastry. Invert the finished pastry onto a lightly buttered baking sheet so that the folds are on the bottom. Brush with remaining egg over the top and sides. Use leftover pastry to decorate the top. Bake in a **preheated** 400° oven until golden brown — about 15-20 minutes. Serve hot with crackers.

TOMATO-FETA SALAD

Serves 6

Combine in food processor or blender until smooth. . .	**1/2**	**cup**	***balsamic vinegar***
	4	**cloves**	***garlic***
	1	**whole**	***lime,*** juice of
	1/2	**tablespoon**	***honey***

With processor running, slowly add. . .	**1**	**cup**	***olive oil***
			salt and pepper to taste

With machine off, add. . .	**1/2**	**cup**	***fresh basil***

then pulse to coarsely chop basil.

To complete this recipe, you will need. . .	**7**	**medium**	***tomatoes,*** thinly sliced
	1	**small**	***red onion,*** thinly sliced
	1/3	**pound**	***feta cheese,*** crumbled

In a medium bowl, place one layer of *tomatoes,* followed by a layer of *onion* slices and then a sprinkling of *feta*. Continue layering in this manner, finishing with tomatoes. Pour the basil vinaigrette over all and marinate for 30 minutes to one hour before serving.

ROAST RACK OF LAMB WITH PEPPERCORN CREAM SAUCE AND JALAPENO MINT SAUCE

Serves 6

We use a mixture of peppercorns — black, white, green, szechaun, pink, etc. Experiment!

For this recipe, you will need...			
	6		***New Zealand lamb racks***
	1	**cup**	***dijon mustard***
	3	**cups**	***bread crumbs***
	1/4	**pound**	***butter,*** melted

Have your butcher take the fat cap off the *racks* and scrape the silverskin from the bones. Brush each rack with *dijon mustard* and roll in *bread crumbs* to coat top and bottom. Arrange the racks on a baking sheet and sprinkle with *melted butter*. Bake in a **preheated** 350° oven until medium rare (about 20 to 30 minutes). Slice racks into chops and serve on a bed of **Peppercorn Cream Sauce**. Pass the **Jalapeno Mint Sauce** separately.

Peppercorn Cream Sauce

A rich homemade stock, with fat removed, is important for the rich flavor of this sauce.

Bring to a boil and reduce to one cup...	10	**cups**	***chicken or beef stock****

In a separate saucepan, combine and bring to a boil...	2	**cups**	***burgandy wine***
	2	**tablespoons**	***brandy***
	1/2	**teaspoon**	***shallots,*** minced
	1	**tablespoon**	***peppercorns,*** coarsely crushed
Reduce sauce by half, then add...			***reduced stock***

Continue to boil until mixture measures 1 cup.

To complete this recipe, you will need...	$^1/_2$	**tablespoon**	***fresh rosemary,*** chopped
	2	**cups**	***heavy cream***
			salt to taste

Add *rosemary* and *salt* to taste. (This sauce can be prepared ahead of time to this point and reheated over medium heat.) Add *heavy cream* and cook over medium heat until thick.

**Homemade chicken stock is a must for this recipe.* *See recipe on page 258.*

Jalapeno Mint Sauce

In saucepan, combine and heat to dissolve sugar...	$^1/_2$	**cup**	***water***
	$^3/_4$	**cup**	***sugar***
	2	**tablespoons**	***green creme de menthe***

Add and bring to a boil...	$1^1/_2$	**cups**	***fresh mint,*** chopped
	3		***fresh jalapenos,*** seeded and chopped

In a separate saucepan, combine and heat to dissolve gelatin...	$^1/_4$	**cup**	***cold water***
	1	**teaspoon**	***gelatin***

Combine gelatin mixture with mint mixture and stir thoroughly. Refrigerate overnight to set. Stir before serving.

NEAPOLITAN CHEESECAKE

Serves 10

Here is a wonderfully delicious and extravagant dessert to wow your dinner guests with! Definitely worth the little extra effort!

To make crust, mix completely and press into the bottom of a 10" springform pan...	$1\frac{1}{2}$	**cups**	***chocolate cookie crumbs***
	$\frac{1}{2}$	**cup**	***butter,*** melted
Double wrap outside of springform pan with foil and refrigerate.			

To make filling, combine and beat until smooth...	$2\frac{1}{2}$	**pounds**	***cream cheese,*** room temperature
	$1\frac{1}{4}$	**cups**	***sugar***

Add, one at a time, beating on low speed...	**6**	**large**	***eggs***

Still beating on low speed, add...	**1**	**cup**	***heavy cream***
Divide mixture into 3 bowls; one with 3-1/2 cups, one with 3 cups, and one with 2-1/2 cups. Set aside.			

In a double boiler, melt...	**2**	**ounces**	***semi-sweet chocolate***

To complete this recipe, you will need...

2	**cups**	***raspberries,*** pureed (fresh or frozen)
1	**ounce**	***Kahlua***
1	**ounce**	***dark creme de cocoa***
2	**tablespoons**	***vanilla extract***

Mix the 2-1/2 cups of cream cheese mixture with the *raspberry puree* until well blended. Pour into the chocolate crust. Bake in a water bath for 20 minutes in a **preheated** 350° oven. Remove from oven and let stand for 5 minutes. **Reduce oven to 325°**.

Combine the melted chocolate, *Kahlua* and *dark creme de cocoa* together and mix well with the 3 cups of cream cheese mixture. Slowly and carefully, starting at the edges, pour this over the raspberry layer. Bake in water bath for 30 minutes in 325° oven. Remove from oven and let stand for 5 minutes. **Reduce oven to 300°**.

Combine the *vanilla extract* with the 3-1/2 cups of cream cheese mixture. Slowly and carefully, starting at the edges, pour this over the chocolate layer. Bake in water bath for 65 minutes in 300° oven.

At this point, the cheesecake should be fairly set in the middle. Leave in the oven for an additional 90 minutes with the oven turned off. Remove from oven and let cheesecake sit out until cooled to room temperature. Then refrigerate overnight before serving.

This cheesecake can be made ahead and frozen. A great timesaver for that extravagant dinner party you're planning! If you choose to do so, simply thaw the cheesecake in the refrigerator for 24 hours before serving.

ADDITIONAL FAVORITE RECIPES

Coconut Chicken Soup

Scampi Vera Cruz

Chef Tim Libassi

COCONUT CHICKEN SOUP

Makes 10 Cups

In large saucepan, combine and bring to a boil...	1	quart	*chicken stock**
	1	tablespoon	*black peppercorns,* whole
	1	tablespoon	*szechaun peppercorns* whole
	1		*lemon,* cut in quarters
Reduce heat and simmer for 15 minutes; strain.			

To strained stock, add...	2	cans	*coconut milk*
	1	pound	*chicken meat,* diced
	2	cups	*mushrooms,* sliced
Simmer for 20 minutes.			

Add and simmer to blend flavors...	3	ounces	*fresh lime juice*
	1	ounce	*tamari or soy sauce*
	1	ounce	*Thai curry paste***
	$1\frac{1}{2}$	tablespoons	*sugar*

In separate saucepan, combine...	$\frac{1}{2}$	cup	*butter,* melted
	$\frac{1}{2}$	cup	*flour*
Cook, stirring constanly, for 5 minutes to form *roux*.			
Add roux to soup, stirring to blend and thicken.			

Serve soup garnished with...			*green onions,* sliced

**Homemade is best (see recipe on page 258), or use good quality canned.*

***Available in specialty food stores or through mail order spice merchants (see page iv).*

SCAMPI VERA CRUZ

Serves 6

This is one of Ned's favorite entrees on the Blue Lion menu; and a favorite with his customers as well.

Instructions	Amount	Unit	Ingredient
In saute pan, over medium high heat, combine and cook for 30 seconds. . .	1 1/2	**tablespoons**	***olive oil,*** heated
	4 1/2	**tablespoons**	***garlic,*** chopped
	1 1/2	**teaspoons**	***ginger root,*** chopped
	5 1/2	**tablespoons**	***jalapeno pepper,*** seeded and chopped

---

Instructions	Amount	Unit	Ingredient
Add and cook for about 3 to 5 minutes, turning once. . .	2 1/2	**pounds**	***shrimp,*** medium size, peeled and deveined

Cook only until shrimp are turning white but are still opaque in the seam along their backs.

Instructions	Amount	Unit	Ingredient
Add and cook over high heat to bring to a boil. . .	3	**cups**	***sherry***

The shrimp should be removed only a moment or two after adding the sherry. Remove them as soon as they are no longer opaque.

Keep them warm while you reduce the sauce to about 3/4 to 1 cup. Remove sauce from heat.

Instructions	Amount	Unit	Ingredient
Immediately add and stir constantly to incorporate. . .	2	**tablespoons**	***fresh cilantro,*** chopped
	1/2	**cup**	***butter,*** cut into small squares

Instructions	Amount	Unit	Ingredient
Arrange shrimp on plates, drape with sauce, and garnish with. . .	2	**whole**	***scallions,*** thinly sliced

the CADILLAC Grille

On the Square
Jackson
733-3279

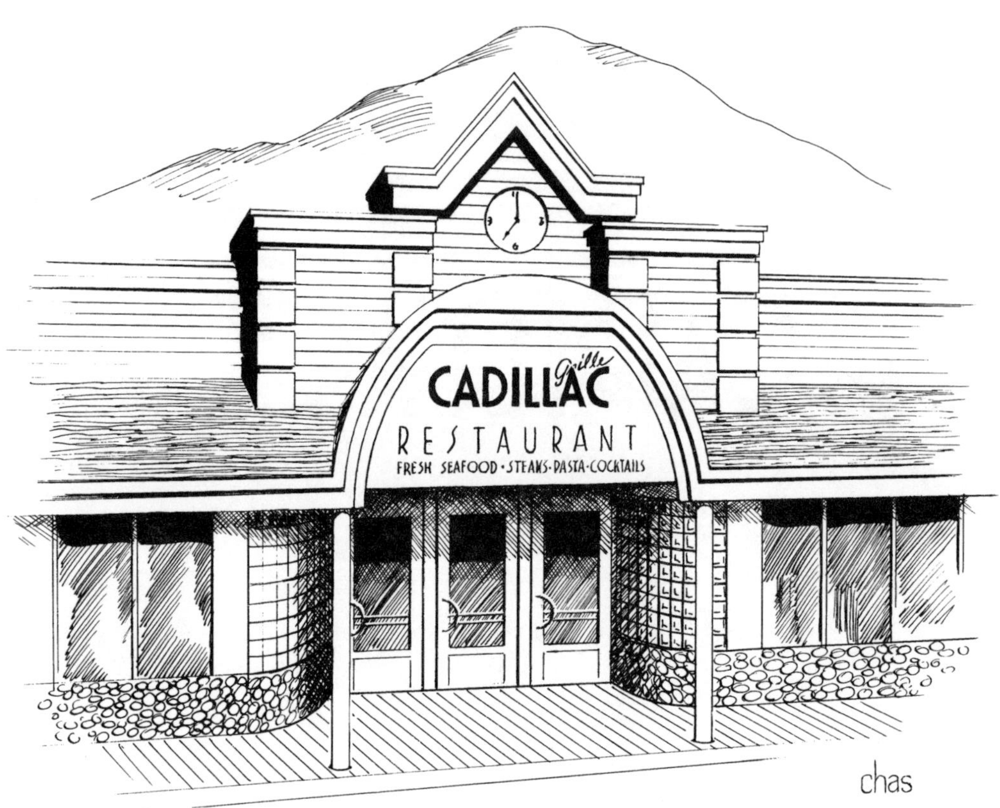

On the west side of Jackson's town square, the Cadillac Grille offers a unique experience for the traveler and resident alike. The moment a person walks through the glass and oak wood doors, he is transported into another era by the award winning 1940's art deco atmosphere. Surrounded by buildings of a predominately western theme, the Cadillac makes a statement with its interior design that includes many art deco influences, such as pink marble flooring, glass brick room dividers and its black and chrome furniture throughout.

The Cadillac offers a very diverse menu of creative cuisine which includes home-made pasta, fresh seafood, lamb and wild game. Chef Suzanne Rominger and her staff will please any palete with their mouth-watering entrees presented in an exceptionally artful and colorful manner.

In addition to its dining room and outdoor patio, patrons can dine perched atop high stools at the black granite table tops in a bar bustling with high energy. From lunchtime straight through the dinner hour, patrons can choose to dine off the regular menu or select a juicy hamburger from the adjoining Billy's Burger diner.

Ken Rominger, along with Suzanne, offer a dining experience to fit any mood. Join them for an afternoon or evening you won't forget! As just a hint of what you might enjoy when dining at the Cadillac, here are three menus with accompanying recipes.

MENU FOR FOUR

Cucumber and Sprout Salad

Firey Malaysian Salmon
with Creamy Leeks

Asian Noodles
with Vegetables

Ginger Creme Brulee

Chef Suzanne Rominger

CUCUMBER AND SPROUT SALAD

Serves 4

Mix together and set aside. . . *(dressing)*	3	**teaspoons**	***soy sauce***
	2	**teaspoons**	***rice vinegar***
	2	**teaspoons**	***sugar***
	1/2	**teaspoon**	***hot chili oil***

Shred. . .	1	**cup**	***European cucumber***

To complete this recipe, you will need. . .	2/3	**pound**	***bean sprouts***
	1/4	**pound**	***bay shrimp,*** cooked

Place shredded cucumber on serving plates, top with *bean sprouts* and finish with *shrimp* on top in the center. Drizzle dressing over all.

FIREY MALASIAN SALMON WITH CREAMY LEEKS

Serves 4

This is a great recipe for entertaining. You can do all your preparation ahead of time, leaving about 15 minutes to cook the salmon and bring it all together.

For this recipe, you will need. . .	**4**	**6 ounce**	***salmon filets***

About 15 minutes before you are ready to serve, cook the salmon by whatever method you prefer — bake, broil, grill, etc. — basting it with the **Firey Malaysian Sauce**. (Take care not to burn the glaze.) A good rule of thumb for proper cooking of fish is 8-10 minutes per inch of thickness; less if you like your salmon a little pink in the middle.

To serve, place the salmon on top of the **Creamy Leeks** and baste the salmon once more with the Malaysian Sauce for added color and flavor; garnish with *orange zest* if you like.

Creamy Leeks

This sauce can be prepared ahead of time and refrigerated. Be careful when reheating the sauce; do it slowly, adding a little more cream if necessary to loosen it up.

Clean well and cut into 2" julienne. . .	**3**		***jumbo leeks,*** white part only

---

In skillet, bring to a boil. . .	**1**	**cup**	***dry white wine***
Add. . .	**1**	**tablespoon**	***shallots,*** minced

Cook for 1 minute over medium high heat to reduce wine by half — about 4 tablespoons should remain.

Increase heat to high and add. . .	**1**	**cup**	***heavy cream***

Cook until sauce has reduced by half and thickened slightly; add leeks and cook until sauce is reduced by half again.

Add and stir to combine. . .	**1**	**tablespoon**	***unsalted butter***
		pinch	***white pepper***
		pinch	***fresh thyme***

Firey Malaysian Sauce

In addition to basting the salmon, this sauce is used to flavor the Asian noodles. It can be made a day or two in advance if you like, then reheated slowly over low heat.

In sauce pan, blend together and boil to reduce by half. . .	**1/2**	**cup**	***olive oil***
	1/3	**cup**	***sesame oil***
	1	**cup**	***white wine***
	1/2	**cup**	***orange juice***
	1/4	**cup**	***honey***
	1/4	**cup**	***light soy sauce***
	1/4	**cup**	***oyster sauce***
	1/4	**cup**	***coconut milk***
	1	**tablespoon**	***hot chili oil***
	1	**tablespoon**	***hot chili paste***
	1	**tablespoon**	***dijon mustard***
	2	**tablespoons**	***fresh mint,*** minced
	1	**tablespoon**	***garlic,*** minced
	1	**tablespoon**	***fresh cilantro,*** minced
	2	**teaspoons**	***fresh ginger,*** minced
	2	**teaspoons**	***red pepper flakes***
	2	**whole**	***green onions,*** finely minced

Reserve a half cup of sauce to baste the salmon. Hold the remainder of the sauce to toss with the **Asian Noodles**.

Asian Noodles

In 4 quarts of lightly salted water, vigorously boil. . .	$^3/_4$	**pound**	***chinese style noodles***

Cook noodles about 5 minutes, until they lose their raw taste but are still firm. Drain the noodles in a colander and rinse with room temperature water, shake dry and gently incorporate *1 tablespoon salad oil* — set aside. (Noodles can be prepared to this point and refrigerated, covered, for two days. **Be sure, however, to take them out of the refrigerator and let them come to room temperature before using them in this recipe.)**

Cut into 2" julienne. . .	**2**	**medium**	***carrots***
	1	**medium**	***zucchini***
	1	**whole**	***leek***
	1	**small**	***red bell pepper***
	1	**small**	***green bell pepper***
	4	**ounces**	***shitake mushrooms***

To complete this recipe, you will need. . .	**2**	**tablespoons**	***salad oil***
	$^1/_4$	**pound**	***bean sprouts***
	$^1/_4$	**pound**	***pine nuts,*** toasted

In a large skillet, heat *salad oil* ; add all julienne vegetables except zucchini and cook quickly over moderate heat about 3 minutes, tossing or stirring vegetables to make sure they do not burn or overcook. Add zucchini, *bean sprouts, pine nuts,* Asian noodles and Malaysian Sauce; stir over heat until noodles are reheated and sauce evenly coats all noodles. (If your noodles have been refrigerated, be sure they are at room temperature so that the vegetables don't get overcooked while you are reheating the noodles — the vegetables should be crisp!)

GINGER CREME BRULEE

Serves 4

In saucepan, bring to a full boil. . .	2	**cups**	***half and half***
	1/2	**cup**	***sugar***
	1	**teaspoon**	***fresh ginger root,*** peeled
Remove from heat, discard ginger and stir in. . .	1	**tablespoon**	***vanilla extract***

In bowl, lightly whip	8	**large**	***egg yolks***

Slowly whisk in half and half mixture. When combined, pour through a fine strainer into another bowl.

To complete this recipe, you will need. . .	4	**tablespoons**	***fresh ginger root,*** very thinly sliced
	8	**tablespoons**	***brown sugar***
	1	**tablespoon**	***ground ginger***

Line bottom of individual souffle dishes with thinly sliced *ginger root* and pour in custard. Put souffle dishes into a shallow baking pan, place the pan on your oven rack and pour about 1 inch of hot water into the pan. Bake the souffles in this water bath at 325° for about 40 to 50 mintues. To test doneness, a knife inserted into the center of a souffle should come out clean.

Before serving, combine *brown sugar* and *ground ginger* and run it through a fine strainer to remove any chunks. Sprinkle this mixture over the tops of the custards and broil briefly to melt sugar to a rich golden brown (watch carefully so that the sugar doesn't burn!).

MENU FOR SIX

Roast Loin of Lamb with Peppered Pecans and Cranberry Salsa

Black Bean Succotash

Peasant Bread

Pears with Fresh Mint and Bourbon Zabaglione

Deno Marcum

ROAST LOIN OF LAMB WITH PEPPERED PECANS AND CRANBERRY SALSA

Serves 6

In a heavy, oven-proof skillet over high heat, sear...	$2^1/_4$	**pounds**	***lamb loin,*** well trimmed

Roast in a **preheated** 350° oven until medium rare (140° internal temperature), for about one hour. Let roast stand a few minutes before slicing. While the lamb is roasting, prepare the sauce.

Saute until golden...	1	**tablespoon**	***olive oil,*** extra virgin
	1	**cup**	***yellow onion,*** diced

Add and simmer for 5 minutes...	$^1/_3$	**cup**	***balsamic vinegar***

Puree in a food processor until smooth. Set aside.

In a separate saucepan, reduce by half...	2	**cup**	***lamb (or) poultry stock****
Combine reduced stock with onion puree. Season with...			***salt and white pepper to taste***

Simmer for 5 minutes. Strain and keep warm (or make ahead and refrigerate, reheating over low heat). Serve the lamb drizzled with this sauce and garnished with **Peppered Pecans.** Pass the **Cranberry Salsa** separately.

**Homemade is best (see recipe on page 258), or good quality canned.*

Peppered Pecans

Combine and toss together. . .

2	**cups**	***whole pecans***
3	**tablespoons**	***unsalted butter,*** melted
1	**teaspoon**	***crushed red chiles***
2	**teaspoons**	***salt***

Spread pecans evenly on a cookie sheet or shallow roasting pan. Bake in a **preheated** 350° oven for 10 to 12 minutes. Drain off any excess butter and let cool.

Cranberry Salsa

Combine and mix well. . .

1 1/2	**cup**	***frozen cranberries****
5	**tablespoons**	***honey***
1/4	**cup**	***cilantro,*** chopped
2-3		***serrano chiles,*** seeded and diced
1		***lime,*** juice and zest of

Pour into a small serving bowl and garnish with whole fresh cilantro leaves. Chill before serving.

**Frozen cranberries rather than fresh are best for this recipe because they are juicier and less tart.*

BLACK BEAN SUCCOTASH

Serves 6

In heavy skillet, over low heat, render...	**7**	**strips**	***smoked bacon***
Remove bacon from pan and discard.			
To bacon grease, add...	**1**	**medium**	***yellow onion,*** chopped
	1	**small**	***red bell pepper,*** diced
	$^1/_2$	**cup**	***Anaheim chili,*** diced
Saute until onion is golden.			
Add...	**1**	**cup**	***black beans,*** soaked
	1	**cup**	***fresh corn,*** cooked and removed from cob
	1	**cup**	***hot water***
Simmer until vegetables are tender.			
Season with...	**2**	**tablespoons**	***butter***
			salt and pepper to taste

PEASANT BREAD

2 Loaves

In small bowl combine. . .	1/4	**cup**	***water,*** 105°-115°
	2	**packages**	***active dry yeast***
Let dissolve 3 to 5 minutes until frothy.			

In large bowl combine. . .	1	**tablespoon**	***sugar***
	1	**tablespoon**	***molasses***
	1	**tablespoon**	***honey***
	4	**tablespoons**	***butter,*** melted
Add yeast and blend.			

Stir in, forming a paste. . .	2	**cups**	***unbleached flour***
	3/4	**cup**	***whole wheat flour***
	3/4	**cup**	***cracked wheat***
	2	**tablespoons**	***salt***

Turn bread paste onto a floured board and knead in. . .	2-3	**cups**	***unbleached flour***
Continue to knead until dough is smooth and elastic – 10 minutes.			
Divide dough into 2 balls and coat each with. . .	1/2	**teaspoon**	***olive oil***

To complete this recipe, you will need. . .	1		***egg,*** beaten
	1	**tablespoon**	***cold water***
	2	**tablespoons**	***coarse cornmeal***

In an area free from cool drafts, allow balls of dough to rise until double in size. Punch each ball down and form it into a round, flat loaf (about 1-1/2" thick). Place loaves on a baking sheet sprinkled with *cornmeal* and allow to rise again to double their size. Using a pastry brush, carefully brush the loaves with the mixture of *egg and water*. Cut slits in the tops of the loaves. Bake in a **preheated** 350° for 40-50 minutes. Loaves should be golden brown and sound hollow when thumped gently. Let rest at least five minutes before serving.

PEARS WITH FRESH MINT AND BOURBON ZABIGLONE

Serves 6

Peel, seed and slice thinly. . .	**3**	**large**	***Anjou Pears***
In bowl, combine. . .	**2**	**tablespoons**	***fresh mint,*** minced
	1	**medium**	***lemon,*** juice of

Toss pears in mint mixture. Let stand for 10 minutes; drain well. Arrange pears in serving bowls or stemmed glasses. Chill well.

In a double boiler, over hot but not boiling water, whisk together until light and fluffy. . .	**2**		***egg yolks***
	2	**tablespoons**	***superfine sugar***

Whisk in, 1 tablespoon at a time. . .	**3**	**tablespoons**	***bourbon***

Beat mixture until it resembles the consistency of a light batter. Remove from heat and continue to whisk until it begins to cool, about 2 or 3 minutes. Pour over chilled pears. Serve immediately.

MENU FOR FOUR

Hazelnut Vinaigrette Salad

Grilled Breast of Duck
with Mango Salsa

Pepper Polenta

Bittersweet Chocolate Torte
with Fresh Raspberries

Chef Suzanne Rominger

HAZELNUT VINAIGRETTE

Serves 4

Mix together and chill. . . *(dressing)*	3/4	**cup**	***champagne vinegar***
	1/2	**cup**	***hazelnut oil***
		pinch	***white pepper***
		pinch	***salt***

Wash, drain well and tear into bite-size pieces. . .	**1**	**head**	***bibb lettuce***

To complete this recipe, you will need. . .	**1**		***fresh papaya or melon,*** sliced
			fresh watercress

Place prepared lettuce into a cloth bag (a pillow case works well) and chill in refrigerator an hour or two before serving to make lettuce cold and crisp! Just before serving, toss lettuce with dressing, place on salad plates and garnish with *papaya* and sprigs of *watercress.*

GRILLED DUCK BREAST WITH MANGO SALSA

Serves 4

For this recipe, you will need. . .	**4**	**whole**	***duck breasts,*** halved
			salt and pepper to taste
			fresh mint leaves *(optional)*

Pat *duck breasts* dry and season with *salt and pepper*. Broil breasts, skin side up, under the broiler for 5 minutes — until skin is crispy but not burnt. Turn over and broil for 3 minutes more. Don't be concerned that the meat is still pink (medium rare) — duck cooks fast and will continue to cook even after it is removed from the heat.

Set breasts aside to rest for 5 minutes, then slice each breast into about 5 or 6 medallions and fan onto a plate — accompany with **Mango Salsa** and garnish with sprigs of *fresh mint*.

Mango Salsa

Peel, seed and cut into 4" cubes. . .	**4**		***mangoes*** *(ripe)*
Peel, seed and mince. . .	**1**	**large**	***red bell pepper***
	1		***fresh anaheim chili***
	1		***fresh jalapeno pepper***

In large bowl, mix together. . .	**1**	**medium**	***red onion,*** minced
	1	**cup**	***fresh mint,*** minced
	1	**cup**	***fresh cilantro,*** minced
	1/2	**cup**	***rice wine vinegar***
	1	**tablespoon**	***fresh lime juice***
	1	**teaspoon**	***salt***
	1	**teaspoon**	***white pepper***

Combine with mangoes and peppers.

Chill until ready to serve.

PEPPER POLENTA

Serves 4

In a heavy saucepan, over medium heat, combine. . .	$1^1/_2$	**cups**	***milk***
	2	**tablespoons**	***black pepper***
			salt to taste

When milk begins to boil, gradually stir in. . .	$^3/_4$	**cup**	***cornmeal***

Lower heat and cook 10 minutes, stirring constantly, until polenta is of a very thick consistency, making sure it does not burn on the bottom.

To complete this recipe, you will need. . .	2	**tablespoons**	***butter***

Spread polenta into a greased 9" x 9" baking pan and let cool. When it is completely cool, cut into 1" squares.

In a large skillet, melt *butter* over medium heat; add the polenta squares and saute 3-5 minutes on each side until lightly brown and crisp. Keep warm until ready to serve.

BITTERSWEET CHOCOLOATE TORTE WITH FRESH RASPBERRIES

Serves 8

In double boiler, melt together. . .	**10**	**ounces**	***bittersweet chocolate***
	6	**ounces**	***unsalted butter***

In large bowl, whip together. . .	**6**	**large**	***egg yolks***
	2/3	**cup**	***sugar***
Gradually add. . .	**1/4**	**cup**	***flour***

In separate bowl, whip until peaks form. . .	**6**	**large**	***egg whites***
	1/3	**cup**	***sugar***
	1/4	**teaspoon**	***salt***

To complete this recipe, you will need. . .

fresh raspberries
powdered sugar

Combine melted chocolate with egg/sugar/flour mixture and mix well. Gently fold egg whites into chocolate batter. Pour batter into a 9" springform pan that has been greased with butter and dusted with dark cocoa. Bake in a **preheated** 350° oven for 30 minutes or until center of cake springs back when touched lightly.

When cake has completely cooled, place a large paper doily on top and sprinkle it with powdered sugar through a fine sieve. Gently remove doily. Serve with fresh raspberries.

Cafe CHRISTINE

Closed

After establishing a catering business in Jackson Hole, Christine Goodman decided to expand her business to include a restaurant. In June 1984, Cafe Christine was born. Serving lunch and dinner, deli style, the restaurant had only 5 tables and a counter with 4 stools. In the beginning, the menu was written on a blackboard and was very small, offering only 4 to 5 entrees a night.

Over a span of 6 years, Cafe Christine flourished to become one of the favorite restaurants in Jackson where locals and visitors dined. Still quite small, with only 8 tables, Cafe Christine offered her patrons an inviting, intimate atmosphere, a menu to please any palate, and a wonderful wine list and full service bar.

During the last three years in business, Christine owed a great deal to her chef, Michael Tepe, who took Cafe Christine's menu to wonderful new heights of culinary experience that kept her customers coming back again and again. Christine gave up her chef's apron and became the baker, creating all the desserts and breads; and she enjoyed being hostess to her customers, making sure their evening was filled with great food and friendly service in a warm and cozy ambiance.

In May 1990, in order to pursue other career objectives, Christine sold the Cafe to Vicky Gouloff. It was a perfect transaction, from one dedicated restauranteur to another.

Over the years, many patrons asked for recipes of their favorite dishes from the Cafe. Here are just a few of those recipes, included in each of the menus offered by Christine and Michael.

MENU FOR FOUR

Shrimp and Scallops in Tomato Saffron Sauce

Spinach Salad with Warm Bacon Walnut Dressing

Pork Tenderloin with Roasted Garlic & Shallots in Brandied Rosemary Demi-Glace

Black Bean Polenta

Tomato and Port Green Beans

Espresso Creme Caramel

Chef Michael Tepe

SHRIMP AND SCALLOPS IN TOMATO SAFFRON SAUCE

Serves 4

Cut into julienne. . .	**2**	**whole**	***green onions***
	1	**medium**	***carrot***
	1	**rib**	***celery***
	1/2	**small**	***red bell pepper***
Place in cold water and set aside.			

In skillet, over medium high heat, combine. . .	**2**	**tablespoons**	***olive oil***
	1	**large**	***shallot,*** minced
	2	**cloves**	***garlic,*** minced
Saute until shallots are transparent.			

Add. . .	**10**	**large**	***sea scallops***
	10	**medium**	***shrimp,*** shelled and deveined
Saute until shrimp are just barely opaque down the center of their spine. Remove shrimp and scallops and set aside.			

To the same skillet, add. . .	**2**	**medium**	***tomatoes,*** peeled and seeded
	1/3	**cup**	***white wine***
Reduce volume by one third and add. . .	**1**	**cup**	***heavy cream***
	1/4	**teaspoon**	***saffron***
Reduce volume by one third.			

Add shrimp and scallops back to skillet, along with. . .	2	**tablespoons**	***cilantro,*** chopped
Cook 1-2 minutes longer to finish cooking shellfish and reduce sauce further. Remove skillet from heat.			
Stir or swirl in until melded into sauce . .	3	**tablespoons**	***butter,*** cold and broken into pieces

Place on individual serving plate and garnish with julienne of vegetables.

SPINACH SALAD WITH WARM BACON WALNUT DRESSING

Serves 4

Rinse and drain well...	2	**bunches**	***fresh spinach***
Place in bowl, cover with damp towel and refrigerate until use.			

In skillet, fry until crisp...	6	**strips**	***bacon***
Pour off and save bacon grease. Crumble bacon.			

In same skillet, over medium high heat, combine...			***crumbled bacon***
	$^1/_4$	**cup**	***walnuts,*** coarsely chopped
	$^1/_2$	**teaspoon**	***black pepper,*** freshly ground
When hot, add...	$^1/_4$	**cup**	***brandy***
Swirl in pan and flame. Cook until flame is out.			

Add...	$^1/_3$	**cup**	***olive oil***
	3	**tablespoons**	***red wine vinegar***
	2	**tablespoons**	***bacon oil***
	1	**tablespoon**	***lemon juice***
	2	**teaspoons**	***dijon mustard***
	1	**teaspoon**	***sugar***
	$^3/_4$	**teaspoon**	***worcestershire sauce***
Cook briefly to combine and heat ingredients.			

Pour over spinach and allow saute pan to cover bowl for 30 seconds. Remove pan and toss well. Serve. (Dressing can be made ahead and reheated before tossing with spinach.)

PORK TENDERLOIN WITH ROASTED GARLIC & SHALLOTS IN BRANDIED ROSEMARY DEMI-GLACE

Serves 4

Most of the preparation for making this dish can be done ahead of time, even the day before, leaving only about 15-20 minutes to cook the pork and bring it all together. Great for entertaining!

In large baking pan, in 450° oven, roast (until soft)...	**16**	**whole**	***garlic cloves,*** cleaned
	12	**whole**	***shallots,*** cleaned
	1	**small**	***green bell pepper***
	1	**small**	***red bell pepper***
The peppers will take about 12-15 minutes; peel, deseed and cut julienne. Garlic and shallots will take 7-10 minutes.			
In skillet, over medium heat, brown until golden...	**2**	**tablespoons**	***pine nuts***

This preparation can all be done the day before. Cool to room temperature before refrigerating overnight. Bring to room temperature before final preparation of dish.

Remove fat and silverskin from...	**2**	**whole**	***pork tenderloins***
Season with...			***black pepper***

In skillet, heat...	**2**	**tablespoons**	***olive oil***
Add, to sear quickly on all sides...			***pork tenderloins***
Remove from pan and place in a **preheated** 375° oven to finish cooking while preparing sauce.			

In same skillet, over medium high heat, add. . .			***roasted garlic cloves and shallots***
			bell peppers julienne
	1	**teaspoon**	***fresh rosemary***
Deglaze pan with. . .	**1/2**	**cup**	***brandy***
Reduce by one half and add. . .	**1/2**	**cup**	***beef demi-glace****

Reduce slightly to thicken.

Remove tenderloins from oven and slice diagonally across the grain. Serve draped with sauce and garnished with roasted pine nuts.

**Homemade is best (see recipe on page 259), or a good quality canned beef consomme which has been reduced to concentrate the flavor.*

BLACK BEAN POLENTA

The day before, in saucepan with 3 cups water, soak. . .	**1**	**cup**	***black beans***

After soaking overnight, bring beans to a slow boil in the water in which they soaked. Reduce heat and simmer until beans are tender, about 1 hour. Allow to cool, drain water and chop to a medium grit. Set aside.

In saucepan, saute. . .	**3**	**tablespoons**	***butter***
	1	**small**	***onion,*** chopped
Cook until onions are transparent.			

Add and bring to a boil. . .	**5**	**cups**	***chicken stock****
Slowly add, stirring constantly. . .	**1 1/2**	**cups**	***cornmeal***
Stir in and mix well. . .			***chopped black beans***
Cook, over low heat, until liquid is absorbed.			

Pour into a greased shallow baking pan and allow to cool before refrigerating for 3-4 hours until firm.

To serve, cut polenta into squares or desired shapes and brown in a skillet or on a grill with a little butter or olive oil.

**Homemade is best (see recipe page 258), or good quality canned.*

TOMATO & PORT GREEN BEANS

Serves 4

Steam until tender crisp. . . (about 10 minutes)	1	**pound**	***fresh green beans,*** trimmed, whole
In skillet, over medium heat, combine. . .			***green beans***
	2	**small**	***tomatoes,*** seeded and chopped
Cook until tomatoes start to soften.			
Add and allow to flame. . .	2	**tablespoons**	***port***
Cook, shaking pan occasionally, until liquid is gone.			
Add. . .	$^1/_4$	**cup**	***fresh basil,*** chopped
Cook 30 seconds longer and season with. . .			***salt and pepper to taste***

ESPRESSO CREME CARAMEL

Serves 4-5

You'll always have room for this wonderfully rich, yet light dessert. Make it the day before you plan to serve it so it can refrigerate overnight. Serve with a dollop of whipped cream!

In skillet, over low heat, melt until golden brown. . .	1/2	cup	***sugar***
Remove from heat and immediately pour equal parts of caramelized sugar into individual ramekins.			
In bowl, whisk together. . .	3	**whole**	***eggs***
	4		***egg yolks***
Beat in. . .	3 1/2	**tablespoons**	***sugar***
Add and mix well. . .	2	**cups**	***half and half***
	2	**tablespoons**	***espresso,*** cold
	1/2	**teaspoon**	***vanilla extract***
	1/8	**teaspoon**	***salt***

Pour gently into ramekins. Place ramekins in a shallow baking pan and pour hot water into pan to come halfway up sides of ramekins. Bake in **preheated** 350° oven for about 1-1/2 hours, until knife inserted in center comes out clean. Cool to room temperature before refrigerating overnight.

MENU FOR SIX

Caesar Salad

Filet Polanaise

Wild Rice Pilaf

Glazed Julienne Carrots

Frozen Lemon Mousse Torte

Chef Christine Goodman

CAESAR SALAD

Serves 6

Cafe Christine was famous for its caesar salad. This recipe, in its original form, makes enough dressing for about 16 large caesars. To the true caesar aficionado, how many croutons, how much parmesan and how much dressing to use is a matter of personal taste. Experiment!

For this recipe, you will need. . .	**1 1/2 - 2**	**cups**	***croutons***
	3/4 - 1	**cup**	***parmesan cheese,*** freshly grated
Wash, drain well and tear into bite-size pieces. . . *(one large handful of romaine for each serving)*	**1-2**	**heads**	***romaine***

It is most important when making a caesar salad that the romaine is cold and crisp before mixing with the dressing and parmesan cheese. Place prepared romaine into a cloth bag (a pillow case works well) and chill in refrigerator 2 hours before serving.

Just before serving, toss romaine with desired amounts of *croutons* and *parmesan cheese* and 1 to 1-1/4 cups of **Caesar Dressing**. Start with the smaller amount of dressing; you can always add more if you like a 'wetter ' salad!

Caesar Dressing

Be sure to make the dressing several hours ahead so it can chill in the refrigerator.

In food processor, puree until smooth. . .	**8**	**whole**	***anchovies***
	8	**teaspoons**	***fresh garlic,*** minced
	1/4	**cup**	***olive oil***
Add and process until well mixed. . .	**2/3**	**cup**	***red wine vinegar***
	2 1/2	**tablespoons**	***dijon mustard***
	2	**teaspoons**	***worcestershire sauce***
	1/2	**teaspoon**	***salt***
	1/2	**teaspoon**	***pepper***
	1/2		***lemon,*** juice of

With processor running, slowly add. . .	$1^3/_4$	**cups**	***olive oil***
Followed by. . .	**3**	**large**	***eggs,*** one at a time

Continue blending for 4-5 seconds after adding the last egg to make sure it is completely emulsified. Chill in refrigerator. Dressing is best at its freshest, for about 3 days.

Croutons*

Cut into cubes. . .	**1**	**loaf**	***french bread***
Sprinkle lightly with. . .			***salt*** ***white pepper*** ***garlic powder*** ***basil,*** dried ***marjoram,*** dried
Drizzle evenly with. . .			***melted butter (or) olive oil***

Bake in a **preheated** 400° oven for 10-15 minutes or until dry and light golden brown. If you want to take the time, browning croutons in a hot skillet (stirring or shaking them often) before baking makes them even more delicious! Easy enough to do if you make a small batch.

**This makes more than you will need for this salad, but they keep indefinitely when stored in a sealed bag or container in the freezer. These croutons are great when used for the Filet Polanaise recipe on the following page.*

FILET POLANAISE

Serves 6

This is a wonderfully elegant and easy main course to make, using the most tender of beef cuts, the filet. Have your butcher cut you the center portion from a whole beef tenderloin — the 'chateau' cut, large enough for 6 persons.

For this recipe, you will need...	**3-4**	**pounds**	***filet of beef tenderloin,*** fat and silverskin removed
Spread evenly over surface of entire filet...			***dijon mustard***
Pat on to coat evenly...			***polanaise crumbs***

Carefully place prepared tenderloin on a baking sheet and bake in a **preheated** 375° oven for approximately 20-25 minutes, or until an internal temperature of 140° for medium rare.

To serve, carefully slice (to prevent dislodging crumb coating from the meat) into medallions.

Polanaise Crumbs

Croutons made from the recipe on previous page, pulverized into crumbs, make the best polanaise crumb mixture. Short of that, use store bought croutons.

In food processor, blend together until well mixed...	**2**	**cups**	***crouton crumbs***
	1	**cup**	***parmesan cheese***
	2	**tablespoons**	***rosemary***
	1/2	**teaspoon**	***garlic powder***

WILD RICE PILAF

Serves 6-8

When roasting the sliced almonds, roast more than you need. It's a shame to waste energy (both yours and the stove's!) for so small amount as is needed here. Roasted sliced almonds are wonderful on lots of foods — salads, desserts, vegetables, etc.

On baking sheet, roast in 400° oven about 8-10 minutes. . .	1/4	cup	***almonds,*** sliced

---

In saucepan, combine. . .	3	tablespoons	***butter***
	1/3	cup	***onions,*** chopped
Saute until onions are transparent.			
Add and saute 5 minutes, stirring occasionally. . .	1	cup	***brown rice***

Add and bring to a boil. . .	1 3/4	cups	***chicken stock****
Cover and reduce to a low simmer for about 50 minutes, until rice is tender and fluffy.			

At the same time, in another saucepan, bring to a boil. . .	2	cups	***water***
	1	cup	***wild rice,*** rinsed twice in hot water
Cover and simmer on low for about 50 minutes, until rice has split and is tender. Pour off any water remaining.			

To complete this recipe, you will need. . .	1/4	cup	***green onions,*** chopped

Combine wild and brown rices, almonds and *green onions*. Serve immediately or keep warm.

GLAZED JULIENNE CARROTS

Serves 6

Cut into 3" julienne. . .	**6**	**medium**	***carrots***
Steam until tender crisp, about 10 minutes.			

In saucepan, over medium heat, combine. . .	**3**	**tablespoons**	***butter***
	2	**tablespoons**	***brown sugar,*** firmly packed
Add and flame with. . .	**1**	**tablespoon**	***brandy***

Cook until flame goes out, then pour over carrots and toss together.

FROZEN LEMON MOUSSE TORTE

Serves 12

In saucepan, combine...	$1^1/_4$	cups	*fresh lemon juice* (6-7 lemons)
			zest of 3 lemons
	1	cup	*sugar*
	2	teaspoons	*gelatin*

Cook and stir over medium heat until sugar dissolves. Remove from heat, pour into large mixing bowl and allow to cool to room temperature.

In another bowl, beat until stiff but not dry...	4	large	*egg whites*

In a separate bowl, beat until medium stiff peaks form...	2	cups	*heavy cream*

Fold whipped egg whites and cream into cooled lemon syrup. Pour into **Mocha Crumb Crust** and freeze for at least 8 hours before serving.

Mocha Crumb Crust

In food processor, puree until fine crumbs...	6	ounces	*chocolate wafers*
	3	ounces	*vanilla wafers*
Add...	$^1/_4$	cup	*butter,* melted
	2	tablespoons	*Kahlua*

Process until well blended. Press crumbs into bottom and partially up sides of a 8" or 9" springform pan. Bake in **preheated** 350° oven for 10 minutes. Cool to room temperature before using. Crust can be frozen at this point for up to two weeks.

DORNAN'S

North of Jackson
at Moose
733-2415

Dornan's at Moose was homesteaded in 1920 by Evelyn M. Dornan. Over the next few years, a grocery store which included a bar, gift shop and gas pumps went into operation. Their famous outdoor Chuck Wagon began in 1948, and has operated ever since, serving breakfast, lunch and dinner every day during the late Spring and Summer months.

In the 1960's, while most people were still looking to the European Continent for fine wines, the Dornan brothers became interested in the wines of Napa Valley, California. They took frequent trips there, bringing many wines back with them. As a result of these trips, the best wine shop west of the Mississippi was born and fine wines were introduced to the State of Wyoming. Their wine shop is a must see for any devotee of fine wines — winner of the Wine Spectator's Award of Excellence for 1989 and 1990.

The bar was moved out of the grocery store to its own location in 1976 and expanded to include a long and winding inlaid-wood bar. Behind the bar are large picture windows spanning two walls through which customers view the Grand Teton — a "stone's throw" away!

During the winter months, the bar is transformed in the evenings with white linen, fresh flowers, candles, and crystal wine glasses adorning the tables to provide an evening of fine dining.

MENU FOR EIGHT

Seafood Squash Chowder

Hearts of Romaine and Grapefruit Salad with Lime Vinaigrette

Herbed Roast Leg of Lamb

Rosemary New Potatoes

Chocolate Creme Brulee

Chef Alton Russell

SEAFOOD SQUASH CHOWDER

Serves 8

This hearty soup, wonderful as an appetizer, can also be served in large steaming bowls as a complete dinner along with a loaf of fresh french bread and a bottle of good chardonnary.

In large saucepan, in 1/4 cup water, steam. . .	**12**	**ounces**	***fresh clams***
	8	**ounces**	***fresh mussels***
Steam only until shells open. Remove clams and mussels from their shells andset aside. Reserve liquid (*clam stock*).			

Cut into 1" cubes. . .	**12**	**ounces**	***red snapper***
	12	**ounces**	***cod or sea bass***
	12	**ounces**	***lobster tail***
	4	**ounces**	***shrimp***
Set aside.			

In stockpot, combine. . .	**3**	**tablespoons**	***olive oil***
	3	**tablespoons**	***soybean oil***
	1/4	**cup**	***onions,*** diced
	1/4	**cup**	***shallots,*** diced
	1/4	**cup**	***red bell pepper,*** diced
	1/4	**cup**	***green bell pepper,*** diced
	1/4	**cup**	***yellow bell pepper,*** diced
	3	**cloves**	***garlic,*** minced
Saute for 5 minutes.			

Add. . .	**1/4**	**large**	***acorn squash,*** parboiled peeled and pureed
	4	**teaspoons**	***fresh ginger root,*** grated
	2	**tablespoons**	***flour***
	8	**ounces**	***tomato puree***
Simmer 2 minutes, stirring constantly.			

Add. . .

		clam stock
$2^1/_4$	**cups**	*chicken stock**
$^1/_2$	**cup**	*dry white wine*
$^1/_4$	**cup**	*dry sherry*
$^1/_2$	**tablespoon**	*parsley,* chopped
$^3/_4$	**teaspoon**	*nutmeg,* freshly grated
$^1/_2$	**teaspoon**	*cayenne pepper*
$^1/_2$	**teaspoon**	*ground allspice*
$^1/_4$	**teaspoon**	*oregano*
$^1/_4$	**teaspoon**	*thyme*
$^1/_4$	**teaspoon**	*cajun seasoning*
		salt and pepper to taste

Simmer 5 minutes, stirring occasionally.

Add. . .

$^1/_4$	**cup**	*yellow crookneck squash,* cubed
$^1/_4$	**cup**	*zucchini,* cubed
$^1/_4$	**cup**	*banana squash,* diced

Simmer 3 minutes.

To complete this recipe, you will need. . .

1	**cup**	*croutons***
4	**whole**	*green onions,* sliced

After simmering the vegetables, add the cubed fish and simmer for 5 minutes. Then add the steamed clams and mussels and simmer another 2 minutes.

To serve, garnish with *garlic croutons* and sliced *green onions.*

**Homemade is best (see recipe on page 258), or good quality canned.*

***See recipe on page 79.*

HEARTS OF ROMAINE AND GRAPEFRUIT SALAD WITH LIME VINAIGRETTE

Serves 8

For this recipe, you will need. . .	**4**	**heads**	***romaine,*** inner, light green leaves only
	3	**whole**	***pink grapefruit***

Wash and dry the inner, light green *romaine* leaves and tear them into manageable-size pieces. Chill until ready for use. Peel and section the *pink grapefruits*, removing all white pith and seeds. To serve, place 3 to 4 sections of grapefruit on top of romaine and dress with **Lime Vinaigrette.**

Lime Vinaigrette

In a food processor or blender combine. . .	**1/3**	**cup**	***lime juice***
			grated rind of 1 lime
	1/3	**cup**	***honey***
	1	**teaspoon**	***onion,*** grated
	1	**teaspoon**	***paprika***
	1	**teaspoon**	***celery seed***
	1/4	**teaspoon**	***salt***
	1/4	**teaspoon**	***dry mustard***
			white pepper, freshly ground to taste

With processor running, slowly add. . .	**1**	**cup**	***light salad oil***

Correct seasoning to taste.

HERBED ROAST LEG OF LAMB

Serves 8

Begin preparation of lamb the day before serving, as it should marinate overnight.

For this recipe, you will need...	**8**	**pound**	***leg of lamb,*** deboned and tied

Combine and saute until translucent...	**1/4**	**cup**	***olive oil***
	1/2	**cup**	***onions,*** diced
	2	**medium**	***shallots,*** diced
	3	**cloves**	***garlic,*** minced
Allow to cool.	**1/4**	**teaspoons**	***salt***

Add and whisk to blend well...	**1/3**	**cup**	***dijon mustard***
	1/2	**cup**	***dry red wine***
	1/4	**cup**	***red wine vinegar***
	1 1/2	**tablespoons**	***soy sauce***
	1	**tablespoon**	***fresh rosemary,*** finely chopped*
	1	**tablespoon**	***fresh thyme,*** finely chopped*
	1	**tablespoon**	***fresh basil,*** finely chopped*
	1	**tablespoon**	***fresh parsley,*** finely chopped*
			salt and pepper to taste
(*1 teaspoon dried herbs may be substituted.)			

While whisking, slowly add in a steady stream until well combined...	**1/4**	**cup**	***olive oil***

Brush the lamb roast generously on all sides with the mustard mixture and let it marinate in a lightly oiled roasting pan in the refrigerator, covered, overnight; or at least for 6 hours. Reserve the remaining mustard marinade.

Let the lamb come to room temperature (allow about 1-1/2 - 2 hours) and brush with reserved marinade. Roast the lamb in the middle of **preheated** 450° oven for 15 minutes, then reduce the heat to 350° and roast it for 1 hour and 15 minutes or until a meat thermometer registers 140° for medium-rare meat. Transfer the roast to a large platter and let stand for 15 minutes, while you prepare the **Wine Sauce.**

Wine Sauce

Pour the fat off from the roasting pan and add...	**1**	**cup**	***dry red wine***
Deglaze the pan over moderately high heat, scraping up the brown bits; boil until it is reduced by half and strain through a sieve into a sauce pan.			

To the saucepan, add and bring to a boil...	**2**	**cups**	***beef broth****

To complete this recipe, you will need...	**2**	**tablespoons**	***unsalted butter,*** softened
	3	**tablespoons**	***flour***
	1/4	**cup**	***brandy***
			salt and pepper to taste

While broth is coming to a boil, combine *butter* and *flour* in a bowl and knead until mixture is well combined. Crumble this mixture, a little at a time, into the boiling broth, whisking all the while. Add any juice that has accumulated on the platter and *salt and pepper to taste.* Simmer for 3 minutes until thickened and add *brandy.* If you want to thicken it further, add 2 tablespoons more of butter, stirring or swirling the pan all the while. Serve sliced lamb with sauce and garnish with fresh rosemary and thyme sprigs.

**Homemade is best (see recipe on page 258), or good quality canned.*

ROSEMARY NEW POTATOES

Serves 8

Wash and cut into quarters. . .	**3**	**pounds**	***baby new potatoes***
In large bowl, mix. . .	$^{1}/_{2}$	**cup**	***olive oil***
	$^{1}/_{4}$	**cup**	***fresh rosemary,*** chopped
	8	**large**	***garlic cloves,*** minced
			salt and pepper to taste

Toss potatoes in mixture to coat well; bake on a shallow roasting pan in a **preheated** 350° oven for 1 hour. Stir occasionally to brown potatoes on all sides.

CHOCOLATE CREME BRULEE

Serves 8-12

A late harvest zinfanel is a wonderful accompaniment to this rich and decadent dessert!

In a heavy saucepan, bring to a boil...	1	**quart**	***heavy cream***
	1/2	**cup**	***brown sugar,*** firmly packed
	2	**tablespoons**	***sugar***

Remove from heat and add...	8	**ounces**	***milk chocolate,*** chopped
Stir until chocolate has melted; allow to cool slightly.			

In medium mixing bowl, whisk until blended...	7	**large**	***egg yolks***
	1	**teaspoon**	***pure vanilla extract***

To complete this recipe, you will need...	1/2	**cup**	***brown sugar,*** firmly packed
			whipped cream, sweetened

Whisk 1/4 cup warm chocolate mixture into the egg yolks. Pour in remaining chocolate mixture and whisk until well blended.

Pour mixture through a strainer into a 13" x 9" x 2" glass baking pan. Place pan in a larger baking pan and add water to the larger pan to come halfway up side of inner pan. Bake 1 to 1-1/2 hours in a **preheated** 350° oven (until a knife inserted in center comes out clean). Cool to room temperature, cover with plastic wrap and refrigerate 6 to 8 hours.

Before serving, pat top of brulee with a paper towel to remove excess moisture. Cover top evenly with *brown sugar* and place under a **preheated** broiler just until sugar begins to melt — about 5 minutes. Watch closely, as sugar will melt very quickly! Serve warm or chilled with *whipped cream.*

Teton Village Road
Across from Teton Pines/The Aspens
733-1886

After 20 years assisting in the operation and managment of family-owned restaurants, Vicky Gouloff carried on her family tradition when she purchased Cafe Christine in 1990 and opened the doors of Gouloff's.

Without changing the cozy, intimate atmosphere, Vicky and her chef, Dan Halstead, have developed their own very distinctive "Teton Cuisine." Gouloff's cuisine features entrees indigenous to the Rocky Mountain region, offering several varieties of game utilizing wild berries, nuts and fresh herbs in distinctive sauces. Pork, fresh seafood, beef, chicken and pasta are other delicious offerings on the menu.

Gouloff's creates all their own delicious and decadent desserts, as well as bakes all their own breads on the premises. A full service bar and a fine wine list add to the dining experience of their patrons and guarantee a wonderful evening!

MENU FOR SIX

Grand Marnier Mushrooms

Golden Corn Ginger Soup

Warm Spinach Salad

Orchard Pork Tenderloin
with Bing Cherry Sauce

Stuffed Acorn Squash

Wild Rice

Sourdough Apple Wheat Rolls

Double Chocolate Torte
with Raspberry Filling

Chef Dan Halstead

GRAND MARNIER MUSHROOMS

Serves 6

In large skillet, over medium high heat, combine. . .	6	**tablespoons**	***butter***
	4	**teaspoons**	***fresh garlic,*** minced
	1	**pound**	***mushrooms***
Saute until mushrooms are softened but still firm.			

Flame with. . .	2	**ounces**	***Grand Marnier***

. . .and stand back!!

Cook a moment or two longer until flames dye off.

GOLDEN CORN GINGER SOUP

Serves 6

*Using fresh Anaheim chiles for this recipe is a **must**! A lot of flavor is lost if you use canned chiles. And if you want a real taste treat, use fresh corn also. An added bonus of this recipe is that it freezes well!*

In skillet, combine and saute until golden. . .	1	**tablespoon**	***butter***
	1	**large**	***garlic clove,*** minced
Add and saute until transparent. . .	1	**medium**	***onion,*** finely chopped
Add and saute until chilies are soft. . .	3	**tablespoons**	***fresh ginger,*** minced
	3	**whole**	***fresh Anaheim chiles*** seeded and finely chopped
Puree in food processor until very fine. Strain through food mill. Set aside.			

Puree together. . .	**8**	**cups**	***frozen corn***
	2	**cups**	***chicken stock****
Strain through food mill.			

To complete this recipe, you will need. . .	**1**	**teaspoon**	***chili powder***
	1/4	**teaspoon**	***cayenne***
	1	**pint**	***heavy cream***
			sugar to taste**
			cilantro (for garnish)

In heavy saucepan combine corn puree with ginger/chile puree along with above *spices* and *heavy cream,* and simmer over low heat for 20 minutes to meld the flavor and color. **Do not boil!** To serve, garnish with a pinch of cayenne and a leaf of cilantro.

**Homemade is best (see recipe on page 258), or good quality canned.*

***Sugar mellows the fire of the spices. The amount of sugar depends on the sweetness of the corn (fresh or frozen). Chef Halstead suggests beginning with 1 tablespoon sugar, adding more if there is a predominant, biting ginger flavor to the soup. It should have a balanced flavor of ginger and corn, with just a hint of sweetness.*

WARM SPINACH SALAD

Serves 6

Rinse and drain well. . .	6	**cups**	***fresh spinach,*** stems removed
Place in bowl, cover with damp towel and refrigerate until use.			
Cut into 1/2" pieces and saute until crisp. . .	1/3	**pound**	***bacon***
Drain bacon on paper towel. Pour out half the fat; return pan to heat, add and saute 1 minute. . .	1/4	**cup**	***olive oil***
	1	**tablespoon**	***shallots,*** chopped
In order listed, whisk in and cook until blended and hot. . .	2	**tablespoons**	***honey***
	1/4	**cup**	***red wine vinegar***
	1	**tablespoon**	***dijon mustard***
			fresh ground pepper
Pour hot dressing over. . .			***spinach***
Add and toss together. . .	1/2	**cup**	***mushrooms,*** sliced
	1/2	**cup**	***bean sprouts***
	2		***eggs,*** hard boiled and chopped
	1	**cup**	***croutons***

Serve immediately.

ORCHARD PORK TENDERLOIN WITH BING CHERRY SAUCE

Serves 6

For this recipe, you will need... **3 whole** ***pork tenderloins***

Butterfly pork tenderloins lengthwise. Place pork between two pieces of plastic wrap and pound with a malet until it is evenly 1/4" thick. (Any good butcher will do this for you.)

In bowl, mix together...

6	**ounces**	***dried apricots,**** diced
6	**ounces**	***dried apples,**** diced
6	**ounces**	***dried peaches,**** diced
1 1/2	**cup**	***walnuts,*** chopped
1/4	**cup**	***brown sugar***
2	**tablespoons**	***honey***
1	**teaspoon**	***cinnamon***

With the rectangle of pounded pork lying horizontally in front of you (so that the grain of meat runs left to right), spread the fruit/nut mixture along the bottom third portion of pork lying closest to you. Starting at the bottom, roll the tenderloin into a log. Carefully, sear the tenderloin in a hot skillet, starting with the seam side first and then carefully rotating the log, making sure not to unravel it, until all sides are seared. If you want, you can tie it with butcher twine to help keep it together while you sear it. Place it seam side down on a roasting pan and bake in a **preheated** 350° oven for 30 minutes. To serve, slice the logs into 1/2" slices and serve on pool of **Bing Cherry Sauce.**

**Del Monte packages these in 6-ounce packages.*

Bing Cherry Sauce

In a heavy saucepan, boil until sugar turns light brown...

1/4	**cup**	***sugar***
2	**tablespoons**	***water***

Add and cook until sugar dissolves...

2	**tablespoons**	***red wine vinegar***
2	**tablespoons**	***raspberry vinegar***
		juice from cherries

Add and bring to a boil. . .	**16**	**ounces**	***dark sweet cherries,*** finely chopped
Mix together and add to sauce . .	**1**	**tablespoon**	***cornstarch***
	1	**tablespoon**	***water***

Cook until thickened.

STUFFED ACORN SQUASH

Serves 6

For this recipe, you will need. . .	**3**	**small**	***acorn squash***

Trim tops and bottoms off each squash and cut them in half; clean seeds from squash and place squash in a pot of cold water. Bring to a boil and cook approximately 20 minutes until just tender. Remove squash from pot and allow to cool. The squash can be prepared to this point and kept refrigerated for a day or two if needed.

Combine together. . .	**1/2**	**cup**	***butter,*** melted
	1/2	**cup**	***raisins***
	1/8	**teaspoon**	***cinnamon***
		pinch	***nutmeg***

Place cooled squash halves, "meat" side up in baking pan and cover with butter/raisin mixture. Bake in**preheated** 350° oven for 15 minutes.

WILD RICE

Serves 6

In saucepan, over medium heat, cook 3-5 minutes. . .	**3**	**slices**	***bacon,*** diced
	1	**small**	***onion,*** diced
	1	**medium**	***carrot,*** diced
	1	**large rib**	***celery,*** diced

Add and bring to a boil. . .	**2**	**cups**	***wild rice***
	4	**cups**	***chicken stock***
	1/2	**teaspoon**	***black pepper***

Simmer over low heat until liquid is gone, about 40 minutes. Toss with fork and serve.

SOURDOUGH APPLE WHEAT ROLLS

Makes 2 Dozen

In saucepan, heat until warm. . .	**1/2**	**cup**	***milk***
	1/4	**cup**	***butter***
	1	**tablespoon**	***honey***
	3/4	**teaspoon**	***salt***

In bowl, combine. . .	**1**	**cup**	***flour***
	1	**cup**	***whole wheat flour***
	1	**package**	***active dry yeast***
	1/4	**teaspoon**	***baking soda***
Add milk mixture and mix until well blended.			

Stir in. . .	**1**	**large**	***egg,*** beaten
	3/4	**cup**	***apple butter***
	1/2	**cup**	***sourdough starter***
Beat on low for 30 seconds, then on high for 3 minutes.			

Stir in. . .	**2-2 1/2**	**cups** ***flour***

Knead dough 6-8 minutes, until smooth and elastic. Shape into ball and place into greased bowl; turn to coat all sides. Cover and let rise in warm, draft free place for 30 minutes. Shape dough into 2" balls. Place on oiled baking sheets, cover and let rise until double. Brush tops with milk. Bake in **preheated** 375° oven for 15-18 minutes, until tops are golden brown.

DOUBLE CHOCOLATE TORTE WITH RASPBERRY FILLING

Serves 12

This is a delicious, decadent cake that looks great too! With the dark chocolate glaze and a white icing spider web pattern on top, it is quite elegant.

In saucepan, over medium heat, combine...	1	**pound**	***butter,*** melted
	2/3	**cup**	***strong coffee***

Add...	**10**	**ounces**	***semi-sweet chocolate,*** finely chopped
	6	**ounces**	***unsweet. chocolate,*** finely chopped
Stir constantly until chocolate has melted and mixture is smooth. Remove from heat and let stand until just warm to touch, about 15 minutes.			
Stir in...	**2**	**tablespoons**	***pure vanilla extract***
Transfer to large mixing bowl and set aside until cool to touch.			

Cream together until light and fluffy (about 5 minutes)...	**12**		***egg yolks***
	2	**cups**	***brown sugar***
	1	**cup**	***white sugar***
	1	**tablespoon**	***molasses***
Fold into cooled chocolate mixture.			
Then fold in...	2/3	**cup**	***flour***

In a separate, clean dry bowl, whip until soft peaks form. . .	**12**		***egg whites***
Mix a third of the whipped whites into chocolate mixture; gently fold in the remaining whites.			

Butter two 10" springform pans. Line bottoms with parchment paper and butter bottoms again. Pour half the batter into each pan and bake in a **preheated** 350° oven for 45 minutes, or until a toothpick inserted in the center comes out with moist crumbs still attached. Cool in pans on racks for about 20-30 minutes before removing from pans. Cakes will fall in the center — don't panic! With a long sharp knife, cut raised edges of cakes to make them level.

To assemble, place one cake on a serving platter and spread **Raspberry Filling** to within a 1/2" of the edge of the cake. Place second cake on top. Spread **Chocolate Glaze** on sides of cake first, finishing with the top.

With **White Icing**, form spider web pattern as follows. Pour icing into a small cone made from parchment paper. Cut off tip to form a small opening. Beginning at center of the top of the torte, carefully pipe an even spiral of icing, spacing the lines about 3/4" apart and ending at an edge. Starting at the center of the spiral design, draw a small sharp knife through icing to the edge of the cake. Repeat the process until you have drawn 8 evenly spaced "lines" through the icing. Now draw the knife from the edge of the torte towards the center, between the "lines" already created. BE SURE to clean the knife before drawing out each line.

Refrigerate torte until glaze is set, about 30 minutes. Serve at room temperature.

Raspberry Filling

In saucepan, combine. . .	**2**	**cups**	***raspberries,*** fresh or frozen
	1/4	**cup**	***sugar***
	1/2	**teaspoon**	***raspberry vinegar***
Cook until the consistency of syrup. Strain mixture to remove seeds.			

Chocolate Glaze

In a heavy saucepan, boil. . .	**$^1/_2$**	**cup**	***heavy cream***
	2	**tablespoons**	***butter***
Remove from heat.			

Add. . .	**5**	**ounces**	***semi-sweet chocolate,*** finely chopped
	3	**ounces**	***unsweetened chocolate***
Whisk until melted and very smooth.			

White Icing

In small bowl, whisk together until smooth. . .	**$^1/_4$**	**cup**	***powdered sugar***
	$2^1/_2$	**teaspoons**	***heavy cream***

At Spring Creek
Top of the East Gros Ventre Butte
733-8833

High atop the East Gros Ventre Butte in Jackson Hole, the Granary Restaurant at Spring Creek offers magnificent views of the Grand Tetons and valley below through its towering cathedral-style windows. In such an awe inspiring ambiance diners have enjoyed breakfast, lunch or dinner since the Fall of 1983. Open year around, the Granary also offers a wonderful Sunday brunch.

In addition to it's fine restaurant, Spring Creek provides condominiums and a hotel along with swimming pool and juccuzi, tennis courts, horseback riding, cross country ski touring, and much more for its guests and residents of Jackson.

Brad Sutton, a graduate of Johnson and Wales School of Culinary Arts and Chef at the Granary, utilizes many of the local and regional products available to provide a delicious dining experience. His menu offers diners the opportunity to taste many different game entrees and appetizers, uniquely prepared. The recipes Brad shares with us are merely a sampling!

MENU FOR FOUR

Pheasant and Duck Pate
with Berry Chutney

Anise Bread Sticks

Spinach Parmesan Soup

Endive, Radicchio and Orange Salad
with Pinenut Vinaigrette

Medallions of Elk
with Morel Port Sauce

Spaetzli

Glazed Baby Carrots
with Leeks

Kahlua Walnut Souffle

Chef Brad Sutton

PHEASANT AND DUCK PATE WITH BERRY CHUTNEY

Serves 4

In food processor, combine. . .	1/2	**pound**	***pheasant thighs,*** boneless and skinless
	1/2	**pound**	***duck breast,*** boneless and skinless
	1	**strip**	***bacon,*** uncooked
Blend until smooth and free of any lumps. Place in large bowl.			

Chop fine and add to pheasant mixture. . .	1	**teaspoon**	***shallots***
	1	**teaspoon**	***scallions***
	1	**teaspoon**	***fresh rosemary***
	1	**teaspoon**	***fresh thyme***
	1	**teaspoon**	***fresh basil***

Add. . .	1	**large**	***egg white,*** beaten
	1/2	**teaspoon**	***salt***
	1/2	**teaspoon**	***black pepper,*** freshly ground
Mix until completely incorporated.			

To complete this recipe, you will need. . .	2-4	**strips**	***bacon,*** uncooked

Line a small pate mold or demi loaf pan with strips of *bacon* and firmly pack mixture inside. Cover with strips of bacon, place mold in a baking pan and pour enough water in the baking pan to come halfway up the sides of the pate mold. Bake pate in this water bath in a **preheated** 300° oven for approximately 1 hour, or until internal temperature is 160°F. Cool to room temperature and refrigerate overnight. Garnish with grapes and serve with french bread.

Berry Chutney

This chutney is also great served with grilled game birds, or pureed to use as a basting sauce.

In skillet, saute over medium high heat until softened...	**2**	**tablespoons**	***unsalted butter***
	1		***shallot,*** minced
Add...	**5**		***plums,*** peeled, pitted and diced
	1/3	**cup**	***raisins***
	5	**tablespoons**	***brown sugar***
	1/4	**cup**	***port wine***
	2	**teaspoons**	***balsamic vinegar***
Simmer over medium heat for 10 minutes, until sauce thickens.			
Stir in and cook another 5-6 minutes...	**2**	**cups**	***blueberries***
Remove from heat and stir in...	**1/3**	**cup**	***raspberries***
			salt and white pepper to taste

Refrigerate until ready to use.

ANISE BREAD STICKS

Makes 2 Dozen

In bowl, combine and mix well...	$1^1/_4$	**pounds**	***flour***
	$^1/_2$	**tablespoon**	***active dry yeast***
	$^1/_2$	**tablespoon**	***salt***
	$^1/_2$	**tablespoon**	***anise seeds***

Using dough hook at low speed, add and mix for 12 minutes...	**6**	**ounces**	***beer,*** room temperature
	6	**ounces**	***water,*** 110° warm

To complete this recipe, you will need...	**2**	**large**	***eggs,*** beaten

Cover bowl with plastic wrap and leave at room temperature for 20 minutes. Cut dough into 24 pieces and, on a floured surface, roll each piece into a stick approximately 12 inches long. Place on greased sheet pan, brush with *egg wash* and bake in a **preheated** 400° oven for 15 minutes or until golden brown.

SPINACH PARMESAN SOUP

Serves 4

In medium saucepan, combine and bring to a boil. . .	**3**	**cups**	***chicken stock****
	1/4	**cup**	***white wine***
	1	**teaspoon**	***lemon juice***
	1	**dash**	***tabasco***

In bowl, combine. . .	**1**	**cup**	***fresh spinach,*** cut into thin strips
	2	**large**	***eggs,*** lightly beaten
	2	**tablespoons**	***fresh parmesan,*** finely grated
Add to stock and bring back to a boil, stirring several times.			
Garnish soup with. . .	**2**	**tablespoons**	***green onions,*** thinly sliced

**Homemade is best (see recipe on page 258), or good quality canned.*

ENDIVE, RADICCHIO AND ORANGE SALAD WITH PINENUT VINAIGRETTE

Serves 4

For this recipe, you will need...

1	**head**	***radicchio,*** leaves rinsed and dry
1	**bunch**	***Belgian endive,*** leaves rinsed and dry
1	**head**	***curley endive,*** leaves rinsed, dry and torn into small pieces
2	**whole**	***oranges,*** peeled and sectioned

On chilled salad plates, place two *radicchio* leaves then three *Belgian endive* leaves fanned in the middle. Place a small mound of *curley endive* in the center, topped off with five sections of *orange*. Drizzle with **Pinenut Vinaigrette** and serve.

Pinenut Vinaigrette

This dressing is best when made the day before you plan to use it.

On sheet pan, in 350° oven, toast until golden brown (about 12 minutes)...

1/4	**cup**	***pinenuts***

Cool completely.

In bowl, combine with pinenuts and mix well...

2/3	**cup**	***olive oil***
1/4	**cup**	***balsamic vinegar***
1/4	**cup**	***fresh lemon juice***
2	**tablespoons**	***shallots,*** minced
1/2	**teaspoon**	***orange peel,*** grated
		salt and pepper to taste

Store in refrigerator until ready to use.

MEDALLIONS OF ELK WITH MOREL PORT SAUCE

Serves 4

For this recipe, you will need...	$1\frac{1}{2}$	**pounds**	***elk loin,*** fat and silverskin removed
	$\frac{1}{2}$	**cup**	***flour***
	$\frac{1}{4}$	**cup**	***clarified butter***

Slice *elk loin* across the grain into eight 3-ounce medallions and pound to 1/4" thickness; dredge with *flour*. In a large saute pan heat *clarified butter* until it almost smokes and sear the medallions on each side for 1 minute; remove from pan.

Add to pan and saute for 2 minutes...	**8**	**whole**	***fresh morels*,*** thinly sliced
	1	**teaspoon**	***shallots,*** minced

Flame and deglaze pan with...	$\frac{1}{4}$	**cup**	***port wine***
Add and reduce until slightly thickened...	$\frac{1}{2}$	**cup**	***game or beef stock*****
	2	**tablespoons**	***heavy cream***
	1	**tablespoon**	***dijon mustard***

Return elk medallions to pan to heat. Serve immediately.

**Dried morels can be substituted; soak in warm water for 15 minutes before slicing.*
***Homemade is best (see recipe on page 258), or good quality canned.*

SPAETZLI

Serves 4

In large bowl, whip until completely blended. . .	**3**	**whole**	*eggs*
	1	**cup**	*water*
	1/2	**teaspoon**	*salt*
	1/4	**teaspoon**	*nutmeg*
	1/8	**teaspoon**	*white pepper*

Slowly blend in. . .	**1 1/2**	**cups**	*flour*

Add flour slowly, until
mixture has consistency of
thin oatmeal. You might
need a little less than 1-1/2 cups.

Place a colander over a pot of boiling water, making sure the colander is at least 4 inches from the boiling water (any closer and the batter will cook before it can pass through the colander). Using a rubber spatula, force the batter through the colander into the boiling water. Cook the spaetzli until they float to the surface; drain immediately and place in cold water until spaetzli are chilled. Drain again and set aside until you are ready for final preparation before serving.

To complete this recipe, you will need. . .	**2**	**tablespoons**	***butter***
	1	**tablespoon**	***parsley,*** chopped

Saute spaetzli with *butter* and *parsley* until heated through. Serve immediately.

GLAZED BABY CARROTS WITH LEEKS

Serves 4

Try to get baby carrots with their tops still on. The greens make a great plate garnish!

In large saucepan, combine and bring to a boil. . .	**2**	**tablespoons**	***white wine***
	2	**tablespoons**	***brown sugar***
	1	**tablespoon**	***lemon juice***
	1	**teaspoon**	***orange zest***
	1/8	**teaspoon**	***cayenne***

Add. . .	**1**	**bunch**	***baby carrots,*** peeled with 1"tops left on
	1	**whole**	***leek,*** split, washed and thinly sliced

Reduce heat, cover and cook for 8-10 minutes, or until done but slightly crunchy. Serve.

KAHLUA WALNUT SOUFFLE

Serves 4

In saucepan, combine. . .	2	**tablespoons**	***butter,*** melted
	$1^1/_2$	**tablespoons**	***flour***
Cook until *roux* just starts to turn golden. . .			

Stirring constantly, add...	$^1/_2$	**cup**	***milk,*** scalded
	3	**tablespoons**	***Kahlua***
Cook and stir until mixture thickens, then stir in. . .	1	**tablespoon**	***walnuts,*** chopped

---

In small bowl, combine and beat well. . .	6		***egg yolks***
	1	**tablespoon**	***sugar***
Blend into Kahlua mixture.			

To complete this recipe, you will need. . .	6		***egg whites***
			sugar

Beat *egg whites* until they are almost stiff, adding 1 tablespoon *sugar* during the last moments of beating. Gently fold the egg whites into the Kahlua mixture and pour into lightly buttered and sugared individual souffle dishes. Bake in a **preheated** 400° oven for 20 minutes. Serve at once.

JEDEDIAH'S *Original* HOUSE OF SOURDOUGH

135 East Broadway
Jackson
733-5671

Popular with locals and tourists alike, Jedediah's was established in 1980. As in the days of the pioneering mountainmen who first brought sourdough to the Rocky Mountain region, Jedediah's uses sourdough starter for all its baked goods. Its sourdough starter is a living organism over 100 years old!

In addition to baked goods, Jedediah's makes all their own jams and preserves, which, along with their starter, all are available for purchase at the restaurant or through mail order (see page *iv* for mail order address).

Jedediah's serves breakfast and lunch all year round. In the summer, customers may enjoy dining on their deck. In place of a dinner menu, Jedediah's is sharing some of their favorite recipes for baked goods.

FAVORITE BAKED GOODS

Sourdough Buttermilk Biscuits

Sourjacks

Coffee Cake

Sourdough Cornbread

Molasses Bran Bread

SOURDOUGH BUTTERMILK BISCUITS

2 Dozen

Combine and set aside...	1/2	cup	*warm water,* (110°)
	1	package	*active dry yeast*
In large bowl, stir together...	4	cups	*flour*
	2	tablespoons	*sugar*
	1	teaspoon	*salt*
	1	teaspoon	*baking powder*
	1	teaspoon	*baking soda*
By hand, crumble into mixture, making marble-size nuggets...	1/2	cup	*shortening*
Add and mix by hand to form sticky batter...	1	cup	*sourdough starter*
	3/4	cup	*buttermilk*
			yeast mixture

Be sure not to overmix. Batter should have small lumps throughout.

On a lightly greased baking sheet, form mounds the size of golf balls. Let sit 30 minutes before baking in a **preheated** 425° oven for approximately 35 minutes, or until golden brown.

SOURJACKS

6 Jacks

Sourjacks are delicious with your favorite jams and preserves. Remember, sourjacks are thin and chewy, not light and fluffy like a buttermilk pancake!

In bowl, combine and whisk well. . .	**2**	**cups**	***sourdough starter***
	1	**large**	***egg***
	1/4	**cup**	***buttermilk***
	1 1/2	**tablespoons**	***vegetable oil***
In separate bowl, combine. . .	**1/2**	**cup**	***flour***
	2	**tablespoons**	***sugar***
	1 1/2	**teaspoons**	***salt***
	1 1/2	**teaspoons**	***baking soda***

Add dry ingredients together with the liquids all at once. Stir lightly. When the batter starts to foam up and double in volumn, stop stirring.

Cook on a moderately hot and lightly oiled flattop or skillet until brown on both sides.

COFFEE CAKE

It's best to have your struesel topping prepared before you make the coffee cake batter.

In bowl, combine...	1/2	**pound**	***butter,*** melted and hot
	1 1/8	**cups**	***sugar***

When sugar is well dissolved, beat in...	1	**cup**	***sourdough starter***
	1	**cup**	***buttermilk***
	2	**large**	***eggs***
	1	**whole**	***lemon,*** zest of

Add and stir to thoroughly blend...	1	**cup**	***white flour***
	1	**cup**	***whole wheat flour***
	1	**teaspoon**	***baking powder***
	1	**teaspoon**	***salt***
	1/2	**teaspoon**	***baking soda***
	1/4	**teaspoon**	***cinnamon***

Pour into a 11" x 15" x 2" lightly greased and floured (paper lined also if you like) baking pan. Sprinkle evenly with **Struesel Topping** and bake in a **preheated** 350° oven for approximately 35 minutes, or until pick inserted in the middle comes out clean.

Struesel Topping

In bowl, combine and mix well...	1/2	**cup**	***pecans*,*** finely chopped
	1/2	**cup**	***sugar***
	1/4	**cup**	***flour***
	2	**tablespoons**	***butter,*** melted
	2	**teaspoons**	***cinnamon***
	1	**teaspoon**	***vanilla extract***

**Oatmeal can be used instead of pecans.*

SOURDOUGH CORNBREAD

In bowl, whisk together. . .	$1^1/_2$	**cups**	***sourdough starter***
	2	**large**	***eggs***
	$^1/_3$	**cup**	***vegetable oil (or) bacon fat***
	$^1/_4$	**cup**	***buttermilk***

Stir in and mix well. . .	$1^1/_4$	**cups**	***cornmeal***
	$^1/_2$	**cup**	***whole wheat flour***
	$^1/_4$	**cup**	***sugar***
	1	**teaspoon**	***salt***
	1	**teaspoon**	***baking powder***
	$^1/_2$	**teaspoon**	***baking soda***

Allow batter to sit in bowl for 20 minutes. Then pour into a lightly oiled 9" x 12" x 2" baking pan. Bake in a **preheated** 375° oven for approximately 20 minutes, or until a pick inserted in the middle comes out clean.

MOLASSES BRAN BREAD

In bowl, whisk together...	1	**cup**	***sourdough starter***
	3/4	**cup**	***buttermilk***
	1/2	**cup**	***molasses*** (preferably unsulfered)
	1/3	**cup**	***vegetable oil***
	1	**large**	***egg***

Stir in and mix well...	1 1/2	**cups**	***bran***
	1	**cup**	***whole wheat flour***
	1	**teaspoon**	***baking powder***
	3/4	**teaspoon**	***salt***
	1/2	**teaspoon**	***baking soda***

Pour into a lightly oiled 9" x 12" x 2" baking pan and bake in a **preheated** 375° oven for approximately 20 minutes, or until a pick inserted in the middle comes out clean.

The Inn at Jackson Hole
Teton Village
733-7102

Named after the Shoshone wife of Richard "Beaver Dick" Leigh, a trapper and settler of Jackson Hole, Jenny Leigh's was established in 1988 in The Inn at Jackson Hole. This pioneering couple was such a large part of the history of the Valley, Jenny Lake and Leigh Lake in the Grand Teton National Park are also named after them.

The menu at Jenny Leigh's Restaurant is unique in its wide variety of wild game, including wild boar! Its dining fare also includes steaks, veal, chicken, seafood, and pasta — for the less 'adventuresome' diner.

Adjoining the dining room is Beaver Dick 's Saloon, its walls adorned with several game mounts of wild animals indigenous to the area. Enjoy a "yard" of draft beer and sports on big screen TV in its relaxed and informal atmosphere.

In addition to the dinner menu in this chapter, which features wild boar as the main entree, owner Bob Kirscher has included in his chapter a recipe for Moose Bordelaise, a favorite entree of patrons who dine at Jenny Leigh's.

MENU FOR FOUR

Avocado with Apple Chutney

Asparagus Salad
with Herbed French Dressing

Roulettes of Wild Boar
with Apricot Sauce

Herbed Baby Potatoes

Fudge Pecan Pie

ANOTHER FAVORITE RECIPE

Moose Bordelaise

Bob Kirscher

AVOCADO WITH APPLE CHUTNEY

Serves 4

For this recipe, you will need. . .	**1-2**		***avocados,*** sliced lengthwise

On chilled plates, fan 3-4 slices of avocado and spoon **Apple Chutney** lightly across the middle of the strips. Serve.

Apple Chutney*

In medium saucepan, bring to a boil. . .	**$1^1/_4$**	**cups**	***red wine vinegar***
	$1^1/_4$	**cups**	***sugar***
	$^3/_4$	**teaspoon**	***ginger***
	$^1/_2$	**teaspoon**	***crushed red chiles***
	$^1/_4$	**teaspoon**	***turmeric***
	$^1/_4$	**teaspoon**	***salt***
	2	**whole**	***cloves***

Remove cloves.

Add and simmer for 30 minutes. . .	**3**	**large**	***green tomatoes,*** seeded and finely chopped
	3	**large**	***granny smith apples,*** finely chopped
	1	**small**	***onion,*** finely chopped

Cool to room temperature, then cover and refrigerate to chill before use.

**Recipe provided by editor.*

ASPARAGUS SALAD WITH HERBED FRENCH DRESSING

Serves 4

For this recipe, you will need. . .	20	stalks	***fresh asparagus***
	1		***red pepper,*** julienne
	1	head	***butter lettuce,*** leaves rinsed and separated

Cook *asparagus* and *red pepper* julienne by steam for about 5 minutes. Asparagus should still be crunchy! Immediately place in **cold** water to chill. Drain and refrigerate until ready to use.

On chilled salad plates, place 2-3 leaves of *butter lettuce* and top with 5 asparagus tips that have been encircled with a "ring" of red pepper julienne. Drizzle with **Herbed French Dressing**.

Herbed French Dressing*

In food processor, combine. . .	1/2	cup	***balsamic vinegar***
	1	small	***garlic clove,*** crushed
	2	tablespoons	***fresh basil,*** (1 teaspoon dried)
	2	tablespoons	***fresh tarragon,*** (1 teaspoon dried)
	2	teaspoons	***dijon mustard***
	1	teaspoon	***salt***
	3/4	teaspoon	***black pepper***

With processor running, slowly add. . .	1 1/2	cups	***olive oil***

Cover and refrigerate until ready to use.

**Recipe provided by editor*

ROULETTES OF WILD BOAR WITH APRICOT SAUCE

Serves 4

For this recipe, you will need. . .	$1^1/_2$	**pounds**	***wild boar loin (or) pork tenderloin***

Butterfly tenderloins lengthwise and place between two pieces of plastic wrap. Pound with a malet until it is evenly 1/4" thick. (Any good butcher will do this for you.)

In saucepan, combine. . .	2	**tablespoons**	***butter,*** melted
	3	**medium**	***granny smith apples,*** chopped
	2	**tablespoons**	***brown sugar***
	$^1/_2$	**teaspoon**	***cinnamon***
	$^1/_2$	**teaspoon**	***lemon juice***

Saute 4 minutes to carmelize.
Allow to cool 5 minutes.

Chop or crush. . .	2	**ounces**	***pistachio nuts***

With the rectangle of pounded tenderloin lying horizontally in front of you (so that the grain of meat runs left to right), spread the carmelized apples along the bottom third portion of tenderloin lying closest to you, then sprinkle with pistachio nuts. Starting at the bottom, carefully roll tenderloin into a log and tie with butcher twine. Brown tenderloin on all sides in a hot skillet. Place seam side down on a roasting pan and bake in a **preheated** 350° oven for 30 minutes. To serve, slice the logs into 1/2" slices and drape with Apricot Sauce.

Apricot Sauce

In saucepan, combine and bring to a boil for 5 minutes. . .	$1^1/_2$	**cups**	***apricot juice***
	$^3/_4$	**cup**	***sugar***
	$^1/_2$	**cup**	***apricots,*** diced
	$^1/_2$	**teaspoon**	***dijon mustard***
Remove from heat and stir in. . .	2	**teaspoons**	***lemon juice***

FUDGE PECAN PIE

For this recipe, you will need...	1		*prebaked pie shell*
			whipped cream
In saucepan, combine...	$^{1}/_{3}$	**cup**	***butter***
	3	**ounces**	***unsweet. chocolate,*** broken into pieces
Stir over medium heat until melted.			
In bowl, combine and beat until blended...	**4**	**large**	***eggs***
	$1^{1}/_{2}$	**cups**	***corn syrup***
	1	**cup**	***sugar***
	$1^{1}/_{2}$	**teaspoons**	***vanilla extract***
		dash	***cinnamon***
Slowly beat in melted chocolate.			
In *prebaked pie shell* spread...	$1^{1}/_{3}$	**cups**	***pecans,*** finely chopped

Pour chocolate mixture over pecans and bake in a **preheated** 350° oven for 50-60 minutes, until center sets. Cool to room temperature before refrigerating. Serve chilled or at room temperature, with *whipped cream*.

MOOSE BORDELAISE

Serves 4

For this recipe, you will need. . .	**20**	**ounces**	***moose sirloin***

Cut *moose sirloin* into approximate 2-ounce cubes. Pound the cubes with a meat mallet into medallions. Dust with flour.

In a skillet, saute medallions over high heat in. . .	**3**	**tablespoons**	***olive oil.***

Add **Bordelaise Sauce** and simmer for 5-7 minutes.

Bordelaise Sauce

In skillet, saute over high heat for 2 minutes. . .	**3**	**tablespoons**	***olive oil***
	1/4	**pound**	***mushrooms,*** sliced
	2	**tablespoons**	***shallots,*** minced

Add and reduce liquid by about 1/3. . .	**1/2**	**cup**	***dry red wine***

Add and simmer 5 minutes, until creamy. . .	**1 1/2**	**cups**	***brown sauce****
			salt and pepper to taste

**Homemade is best (see recipe on page 260), or good quality canned.*

At The Wort
Broadway & Glenwood
733-2190

The Wort Hotel shares a vital part in the history of Jackson Hole. Originally built in 1941 by the Wort Brothers, it has seen many changes through the years. JJ's Silver Dollar Bar and Grill, at the Wort, is famous for its bar inlaid with 2,032 silver dollars, reflecting its gambling heyday and reminding us of the rough and tumble days of the cowboys and ranchers who spent their Saturday nights in town "bellied up to the bar." Those days are gone, but the romance of the cowboy and the Old West still remain at the Wort!

JJ's Silver Dollar Bar and Grill offers refreshment and dining in comfortable luxury to its guests and residents alike in this elegant hotel in the heart of downtown Jackson. Its inviting atmosphere is rich in the history of days gone by, evidenced by the photos and memorbilia along the walls in the restaurant and lobby areas.

The only AAA Four-Diamond hotel in Jackson, the Wort has 60 spacious rooms, along with complete conference facilities, services and personal attention for groups of up to 100.

Chef Alan Myers, raised on cattle ranches and still a country boy at heart, has spent 18 years perfecting what he refers to as a "western elegance" style of cooking. He focuses on regional cuisine that is wholesome and hearty.

MENU FOR FOUR

Veal Consomme Julienne

***Mixed Greens
with Marinated Mozzarella Cheese
and Walnuts***

Orange Sorbet

***Loin of Elk
with Morel Mushrooms and
Apricot Demi-Glace***

Duchess Potatoes

Fresh Green Beans

Huckleberry Cake

Chef Alan Myers

VEAL CONSOMME JULIENNE

Serves 4

As the base for this soup, you must first make a veal stock.

In large stockpot, combine... *(veal stock)*	1	gallon	***water***
	$6^1/_2$	pounds	***veal bones,*** rinsed to remove excess blood
	$1^1/_2$	pounds	***beef bones,*** rinsed
	$^1/_3$	pound	***celery,*** chopped
	$^1/_3$	pound	***leeks,*** chopped
	$^1/_3$	pound	***onions,*** chopped

Combine in cheese cloth, tie and place in stock...	10	whole	***black peppercorns***
	3	whole	***cloves***
	2	whole	***bay leaves***
	1	sprig	***fresh thyme***
	1	sprig	***fresh parsley***

Bring stock to a boil then reduce to a simmer for 8 hours. Strain stock through cheese cloth and cool. When cooled, skim off fat. Yield should be approximately 2-1/2 quarts.

In stockpot, combine...			***veal stock***
	$1^1/_2$	pounds	***round of beef,*** lean with no fat, chopped
	$^1/_2$	cup	***chicken giblets,*** finely chopped
	1	small	***carrot,*** finely chopped
	3		***leeks,*** white part only, finely chopped
	1	large	***egg white***

Bring slowly to a boil; reduce heat and simmer partially covered for 90 minutes. Strain through cheese cloth, which has been soaked beforehand in tepid water and wrung out, into another saucepan. Consomme should be clear. Reheat before serving.

To serve, ladle into serving bowls and add 1 teaspoon each of fine julienne cut *carrots, celery, white part of leeks and turnips.* Bread sticks are a nice accompaniment.

MIXED GREENS WITH MARINATED MOZZARELLA CHEESE

To achieve the flavor of this salad at its best, you must marinate the mozzarella cheese for a week before final preparation.

Cut into 1/2" x 1/2" strips. . .	1/2	**pound**	***mozzarella cheese***
Marinate for 1 week in. . .	**1**	**cup**	***raspberry vinegar***

Wash, drain well and tear into bite-size pieces. . .

(enough for 4 persons)

assorted greens, i.e. bib, butter, radicchio watercress, etc.
assorted fresh herbs, i.e. tarragon, thyme, mint, basil, etc.

Toss greens and herbs with. . .	1/2	**cup**	***olive oil***
	1/2	**cup**	***raspberry vinegar*** (which cheese has marinated in)
To complete this recipe you will need. . .	**1**	**cup**	***walnuts,*** chopped

Place greens on chilled plates and top with *mozzarella* strips and chopped *walnutss*

ORANGE SORBET

Serves 4

In saucepan, combine...	1/2	**cup**	***water***
	3/4	**cup**	***sugar***
	1	**teaspoon**	***unflavored gelatin***
Stir over medium heat until dissolved.			

Add and stir to blend...	1 1/2	**cups**	***fresh orange juice,*** strained
	1	**teaspoon**	***orange rind,*** finely grated

Place in pan and freeze for approximately 2 hours or until mushy-firm. Break up and beat in chilled bowl with electric beater until fluffy. Store in covered container in freezer.

To complete this recipe,
you will need...

champagne (or)
lemon lime soda
fresh mint leaves

Using small scoop, serve sorbet in champagne glasses topped off with *champagne* or *lemon lime soda* and garnished with *fresh mint leaves.*

LOIN OF ELK WITH MOREL MUSHROOMS AND APRICOT DEMI-GLACE

Serves 4

With the apricot demi-glace made ahead of time, your final preparation of this dish should only take about 30 minutes.

For this recipe, you will need...	2	**pounds**	***elk loin,*** fat and silverskin removed
	1/2	**cup**	***flour***
	1/4	**cup**	***clarified butter***
			salt and pepper

Slice the *elk loin* across the grain into 2" to 2-1/2" medallions. Dust with flour seasoned to taste with *salt and pepper*. In a large saute pan heat *clarified butter* until it is quite hot and sear the medallions for approximately 1 minute on each side; remove from pan and keep warm.

Add to pan and saute for 1 minute...	1	**pound**	***fresh morels*,*** thinly sliced
Flame and deglaze pan with...	1/4	**cup**	***brandy***

Reduce brandy by half; add **Apricot Demi-Glace** and simmer briefly. Serve elk medallions draped with sauce.

**Shitaki mushrooms make an excellent substitute. Dried mushrooms of either type can be substituted. Soak in warm water for 15 minutes before slicing.*

Apricot Demi-Glace

For this recipe, you will need...	1/2	**pound**	***dried apricots,*** cut julienne
	1/2	**cup**	***apricot brandy***
	3	**cups**	***brown sauce****

Soak apricot julienne in brandy for 1 hour. Place in sauce pan and bring to a boil. Add brown sauce and simmer over low heat for 30 minutes.

**Homemade is best (see recipe on page 260), or a good quality canned.*

HUCKLEBERRY CAKE

Huckleberries are reminiscent of blueberries, but much smaller and sweeter. During the month of August, the mountains around Jackson are abundant with them.

In bowl, cream together until fluffy. . .	$^{1}/_{2}$	cup	***butter,*** softened
	1	cup	***sugar***
Add and beat until well blended. . .	3	large	***eggs***
	$^{3}/_{4}$	cup	***milk***
Sift together and combine with mixture. . .	$2^{1}/_{4}$	cups	***flour***
	2	teaspoons	***baking powder***
Beat until smooth.			
Gently stir in. . .	1	cup	***huckleberries,*** dredged in flour

Pour into springform or deep cake pan and bake in **preheated** 350° oven for 30 minutes or until center of cake springs back when touched lightly. Cool in the pan on a rack for 15 minutes; remove from pan and top with **Glaze**. Cool completely.

Serve slices of cake on a pool of **Huckleberry Sauce** and garnish with whipped cream.

Glaze

Combine, over low heat, until mixture comes to a boil. . .	$^{1}/_{2}$	cup	***honey***
	1	cup	***powdered sugar***

Huckleberry Sauce

Puree in food processor. . .	1	pint	***huckleberries***
	5	tablespoons	***sugar***

On the Square
In the Million Dollar Cowboy Bar
733-4790

La Chispa Restaurant first opened its doors in 1982 and has been serving authentic mexican food ever since. According to owner, Bob Melcer, their recipes "are a conglomeration of years of research, trial and error, and indigestion!" Many of their recipes are similar to those found in the province of Jalesco, in central Mexico.

"Mexican food should always be fun to prepare and serve. We have tried to provide recipes here that will be fun. These recipes can be used exactly as printed, or as a guideline, adding your own ideas and flair. Good results will be easily attainable.

Good luck, and don't forget the margaritas!!

MENU FOR FOUR

Nachos with Guacamole

Margarita Chicken

Chiles Rellenos Con Queso

Mexican Rice

Sopapillas

Chef Bob Melcer

NACHOS WITH GUACAMOLE

Serves 4

For this recipe, you will need...

1	**bag**	***corn tortilla chips***
1	**pound**	***cheddar and/or jack cheese,*** grated
1	**can**	***jalapenos,*** sliced

Spread *corn tortilla chips* on oven-proof plate and top generously with grated *cheese*. Place under broiler for approximately 2 minutes to melt cheese. Sprinkle with *jalapenos* and **Guacamole**.

Guacamole

In bowl, combine and smash together...

2	**large**	***avocados*,*** (ripe), cored and peeled
1/4	**cup**	***onion,*** minced
1/4	**cup**	***green onion,*** chopped
1	**tablespoon**	***olive oil***
1	**teaspoon**	***garlic,*** minced
1	**teaspoon**	***chili pepper***
1	**teaspoon**	***salt***

Cover and set stand for 1-2 hours before serving.

**Hass avocados are best!*

MARGARITA CHICKEN

Serves 4

For this recipe, you will need. . .	4	whole	***chicken breasts,*** boned and skinned

In bowl, combine. . .	2	whole	***oranges,*** juice of
(marinade)	2	whole	***limes,*** juice of
	$1/4$	cup	***honey***
	$1/4$	cup	***tequila***
	2	tablespoons	***triple sec***
	1	teaspoon	***salt***

To complete this recipe, you will need. . .	1	cup	***guacamole***
	1	cup	***sour cream***
	1	whole	***orange,*** cut into wedges
	1	whole	***lime,*** cut into wedges

Soak *chicken breasts* in marinade for at least 2 hours. Grill or broil chicken breasts for aproximately 4-5 minutes per side. Serve with *guacamole, sour cream* and **Salsa Baracha**; garnish with lime and orange wedges.

Salsa Baracha

In bowl, combine. . .	2	cups	***tomatoes,*** diced
	$1/4$	cup	***onion,*** chopped
	$1/4$	cup	***green onion,*** chopped
	1	whole	***jalapeno,*** diced
	1	tablespoon	***cilantro,*** chopped
	1	tablespoon	***tequila***
	1	teaspoon	***Mexican oregano***
	1	teaspoon	***salt***
	1	whole	***lime,*** juice of

Cover and refrigerate for about 2 hours before serving to meld flavors.

CHILES RELLENOS CON QUESO

Serves 4

For this recipe, you will need...	2	**7 oz. cans**	*green chiles*
	1/4	**pound**	*monterey jack cheese*
	1	**cup**	*flour*

Drain and seed *chiles*. Stuff each chile with a strip of *jack cheese* 1/2" x 1" x 2" and roll in flour to coat all over. Set aside.

Beat until very stiff and dry...	4		*egg whites*
Gently fold in...	4		*egg yolks,* slightly beaten

To complete this recipe, you will need...	**2-3**	**cups**	*vegetable oil*

In skillet heat 1/2" deep *vegetable oil* to 350°. Coat chiles with egg batter and carefully set into oil with spatula. Cook for 2 minutes on both sides. Place rellenos on oven-proof platter, top with **Relleno Salsa** and bake in **preheated** 350° oven for 12 minutes. Serve immediately.

Relleno Salsa

In skillet, saute until tender...	1	**cup**	*onion,* finely minced
	1	**tablespoon**	*garlic,* finely minced
	2	**tablespoons**	*vegetable oil*

Add and simmer for 1 hour...	2	**cups**	*tomatoes,* diced
	2	**cups**	*green chiles,* diced
	2	**cups**	*chicken broth*
	1	**teaspoon**	*white pepper*
	1	**teaspoon**	*cumin*
	1	**teaspoon**	*chile powder*
	1	**teaspoon**	*Mexican oregano*
	2	**whole**	*bay leaves*

MEXICAN RICE

Serves 4

In saucepan, over high heat,			
saute until brown. . .	**1**	**cup**	*white rice*
(it takes a while)	**2**	**tablespoons**	*vegetable oil*

Add. . .	**2**	**cups**	*water*
	1/2	**cup**	*onions,* chopped
	1/2	**cup**	*green onions,* chopped
	1/2	**cup**	*tomatoes,* chopped
	1/4	**cup**	*parsley,* chopped
	1	**tablespoon**	*fresh garlic,* minced
	1	**teaspoon**	*salt*
	1	**teaspoon**	*white pepper*

Cover and cook over low heat until all liquid is absorbed (about 40 minutes).

Fluff with fork and serve.

SOPAPILLAS

Serves 4

In bowl, combine. . .	**1**	**cup**	***water,*** warm (110°)
	1/2	**cup**	***sugar***
	1	**package**	***dry active yeast***
Allow to stand 5 minutes.			

In another bowl, mix together. . .	**2**	**cups**	***flour***
	1	**tablespoon**	***cinnamon***

To complete this recipe, you will need. . .	**3-4**	**cups**	***vegetable oil***
	1	**cup**	***honey***

Combine flour and yeast mixture together; knead for 5 minutes. Allow dough to rise in a warm, draft-free place until double in size, about 40 minutes. Roll dough out to a rectangle shape approximately 1/4" thick. Cut out 4" triangles.

In skillet, heat 3/4" deep *vegetable oil* to 335°. Cook triangles of dough in hot oil on each side until golden brown. Let cool. Serve drizzled with *honey*.

LAME DUCK CHINESE RESTAURANT

680 East Broadway
Jackson
733-4311

Joe and Sylvia Diprisco have owned the Lame Duck Chinese Restaurant for the past 10 years. Not possessing any real practical or professional training in oriental cooking was cause for a rocky start. By employing the services of Florence Lin, a well-known teacher and cookbook author, they were able to bridge the rough spots.

A trip to Hong Kong for several weeks of instruction in a Chinese cooking school (with interpreter!) gave Joe the expertise he needed to create a menu of authenticity with a wide assortment of dishes, including some Chinese, Hunan, and Szechuan. Another trip, to Tahiti, was responsible for a tropical influence to the Lame Duck's atmosphere and the introduction of tropical drinks.

Two of their most popular features of the restaurant are their authentic tea rooms for private parties and their Tahitian grass hut for small groups.

Joe and his staff offer Sushi and Sashimi and don't think twice about borrowing ideas or ingredients from any kind of cuisine they want to. Thus, when you try these recipes or come to Jackson, you'll know why they say, "Don't miss the Lame Duck difference!"

MENU FOR FOUR

Perfume Chicken

Hot and Sour Soup

Wyoming Rolls

Samaurai Shrimp
with Mushu Pancakes

Tea Smoked Chicken

Malaysian Fried Rice

Chef Joe Diprisco

PERFUME CHICKEN

Serves 4

Begin this dish the day before so you can marinate the cucumber overnight.

Seed and cut into julienne strips. . .	1	**whole**	***cucumber***
In mixing bowl, combine. . .	2	**cups**	***white vinegar***
(marinade)	1	**tablespoon**	***green onion,*** minced
	1	**tablespoon**	***fresh ginger,*** grated
	$1^1/_2$	**teaspoons**	***sesame oil***
Add cucumber julienne to marinade, cover and refrigerate overnight.			

In saucepan, combine. . .	$4^1/_2$	**ounces**	***chili sauce***
(sauce)	3	**ounces**	***soy sauce***
	$1^3/_4$	**ounces**	***rice vinegar***
	$1^3/_4$	**ounces**	***sesame oil***
	2	**tablespoons**	***white wine***
	3	**teaspoons**	***sugar***
	$1^1/_2$	**teaspoons**	***Thai chili garlic paste****
Simmer for 10 minutes. Allow to cool.			

Steam, over medium heat for 15 minutes, until just done. . . (don't over cook!)	8	**ounces**	***chicken breast,*** boneless and skinless
Cool and cut into julienne strips. Set aside.			

To complete this recipe, you will need. . .	2	**cups**	***cabbage,*** shredded
	2	**tablespoons**	***sesame seeds***

To serve, place bed of *cabbage* on platter; add a layer of cucumbers over cabbage, then a layer of chicken, top with sauce and sprinkle lightly with *sesame seeds.*

**Available in specialty food stores or through mail order spice merchants (see page iv).*

HOT AND SOUR SOUP

Makes 2 Quarts

In large saucepan, combine and heat. . .	8	**cups**	***chicken stock,*** clear
	3	**ounces**	***red wine vinegar***
	2	**tablespoons**	***soy sauce***
	1	**tablespoon**	***Thai chili garlic paste****
Add and bring to a gentle boil. . .	3	**whole**	***black mushrooms*,*** soaked in hot water then sliced
	1/2		***lily flowers*,*** soaked in hot water then sliced
In bowl, mix together. . .	1/2	**cup**	***water***
	1/4	**cup**	***cornstarch***
Slowly add to soup, stirring constantly.			
To complete this recipe, you will need. . .	2	**whole**	***eggs,*** whipped
	4	**whole**	***green onions,*** chopped

Turn heat down and allow soup to clarify. With heat on low, slowly dribble in *whipped eggs* and allow to cook. Serve garnished with *green onions*.

**Available in specialty food stores or through mail order spice merchants (see page iv).*

WYOMING ROLLS

Serves 4

Our western version of the popular nori rolls, Lame Duck's contribution to the world of sushi!

For this recipe, you will need. . .	**1**	**pound**	***trout***
In bowl, combine. . .	**$1^1/_2$**	**cups**	***whole tea leaves****
	$^3/_4$	**cup**	***rice,*** uncooked
	$^1/_2$	**cup**	***brown sugar***
	3-4	**pieces**	***star anise****

Line bottom of wok with aluminum foil, then spread tea leaf mixture on top of foil. Place a metal rack in wok so there is an air space between mixture and rack. Lightly oil rack and lay trout on it. Cover wok with wok cover and turn heat on high for approximately 1 minute; then turn heat down to medium for 15 minutes. When 15 minutes is up, turn heat off **but leave wok covered for 10 minutes more.** Don't peek! When 10 minutes is up, remove trout, allow to cool to room temperature, then chill in refrigerator until ready to use.

In saucepan, combine. . .	**$1^1/_2$**	**cups**	***water***
	1	**cup**	***short grain white rice,*** rinsed twice with cold water
	1	**teaspoon**	***mirin vinegar****

Bring to a boil, cover and simmer over low heat for 10-12 minutes.

In small bowl, combine. . .	**2**	**tablespoons**	***rice wine vinegar***
	$^3/_4$	**teaspoon**	***sugar***
	$^1/_2$	**teaspoon**	***salt***

Add to cooked rice while fluffing with fork. Let rice cool to room temperature. This is *sushi rice.*

To complete this recipe,
you will need. . .

4	**sheets**	***nori wrappers**** (seaweed wrapper)
$^1/_2$		***avocado,*** peeled, pitted and sliced
		soy sauce
		wasabi*
		pickled ginger*, sliced
		bamboo sushi roller*

One at a time, place a *nori wrapper* (with 1-1/2" trimmed off any side) on *bamboo roller* and cover with *sushi rice,* leaving 1" along one side uncovered. Slice smoked trout into strips and lay a couple of strips across the width of rice-covered nori wrapper. Place strips of *avocado* next to trout. Using bamboo roller and starting with rice-covered edge of nori wrapper, roll seaweed towards bare edge of wrapper keeping the roll tight with even pressure; and along the way, enveloping the trout and avocado strips. When roll is completely wrapped to the bare edge, wet this edge with water or vinegar and press it against the roll to seal edge. Cut roll into 8-10 pieces and serve with *soy sauce, wasabi,* and *pickled ginger.*

**Available in specialty food stores or through mail order spice merchants (see page iv).*

SAMAURAI SHRIMP WITH MUSHU PANCAKES

Serves 4

Lame Duck's version of the Mexican Fajita — it's a hot one! You will want to have a variety of sauces on hand to serve with this; hoisin, plum, sweet and sour, etc. ***Mushu pancakes*** *can be purchased frozen in specialty stores and Chinese markets. This dish is also wonderful made with chicken.*

In small bowl, combine. . .	1/2	**cup**	***chicken stock***
(sauce)	1/4	**cup**	***soy sauce***
	2	**tablespoons**	***white wine***
	2	**tablespoons**	***oyster sauce***
	1 1/2	**teaspoons**	***sugar***
	1	**whole**	***star anise***
	1	**pinch**	***white pepper***
Set aside.			

In wok, heat. . .	2	**tablespoons**	***soy bean oil,*** heated
then add. . .	1/2	**pound**	***shrimp,*** cleaned and deveined
	1	**cup**	***yellow onions,*** sliced
Cook until shrimp are just barely opaque down the center of its spine. Remove shrimp and onions; set aside.			

Clean wok, add more oil and. . .	1	**cup**	***bamboo shoots***
	1	**cup**	***cabbage,*** shredded
	1	**whole**	***red bell pepper,*** cut in strips
	1	**whole**	***green bell pepper,*** cut in strips
	6	**ounces**	***Chinese longbeans,*** blanched
Stir-fry until vegies are half done.			

Add shrimp and onions back to wok, along with. . .	2	**teaspoons**	***crushed chili peppers***
	1	**teaspoon**	***garlic,*** minced
	1/2	**teaspoon**	***fresh ginger,*** grated

Stir-fry about 1 minute, then add the *sauce* you prepared earlier and stir-fry 30 seconds longer. Serve with mushu pancakes and sauces you enjoy, i.e. hoisin, plum, sweet and sour.

TEA SMOKED CHICKEN*

Serves 4

This is a very popular dish at the Duck and sells out every time it's on special. Preparation should begin the day before, as the chicken must marinate overnight before roasting and smoking it.

For this recipe, you will need. . .	1	**whole**	***chicken***
	1/4	**cup**	***green onions,*** chopped
	3-4	**tablespoons**	***fresh ginger,*** grated
	1/4	**cup**	***soy sauce***

Ground *green onions* and *ginger* together and rub the chicken inside and out. Refrigerate overnight. Roast chicken in a **preheated** 325° oven for 45 minutes. Do not overcook! Allow chicken to cool down, then rub skin with *soy sauce.*

In bowl, combine. . .	1 1/2	**cups**	***whole tea leaves****
	3/4	**cup**	***rice,*** uncooked
	1/2	**cup**	***brown sugar***
	3-4	**whole**	***star anise****

Line bottom of wok with aluminum foil and spread tea leaf mixture on top of foil. Place a metal rack in wok so there is an air space between the mixture and rack. Lightly oil rack and place chicken on it. Cover wok with wok cover and turn heat on high for approximately 1 minute; then turn heat down to medium for 15 minutes. When 15 minutes is up, turn heat off **but leave wok covered for 10 minutes more.** Don't peek! When 10 minutes is up, remove chicken. You can serve immediately or allow chicken to cool to room temperature and chill in refrigerator if you won't be serving it until the next day or for several hours. If you allow it to cool or chill, reheat it in a 350° oven for about 10-15 minutes before serving.

To serve, cut chicken in half, then chop each half into pieces and place the pieces of chicken on a platter as though the chicken half were still one piece.

**Editor's Note: I have had this and it is <u>scrumptious</u> -- worth any effort to make it!!*

MALAYSIAN FRIED RICE

Serves 4-6

Preparation for this side dish should begin the day before, as the rice must be cooked and then allowed to dry before the final cooking process takes place.

The **day before** serving this dish, in saucepan, combine...	$4^1/_2$	**cups**	***water***
	3	**cups**	***short grain white rice,*** rinsed twice with cold water

Bring to a boil, cover and simmer over low heat 10-12 minutes. Spread cooked rice out on a sheet pan to come to room temperature and dry. Store covered in refrigerator over night.

In wok, combine...	2	**tablespoons**	***soy bean oil,*** heated
	4	**ounces**	***beef round steak,*** chopped small
	4	**ounces**	***baby shrimp***
Cook for 1 minute.			

Add...	$^3/_4$	**cup**	***cabbage,*** shredded
	$^1/_2$	**cup**	***green onions,*** chopped
	1	**tablespoon**	***garlic,*** chopped
	2	**teaspoons**	***crushed red chilis***
	1	**teaspoon**	***shrimp paste***
Cook for 1 minute.			

Add...			***cooked rice***
	$^1/_2$	**cup**	***eggs,*** hard cooked and chopped
Stir-fry mixture until rice is hot and ingredients are mixed together well.			

Add...	3	**tablespoons**	***soy sauce***
	1	**teaspoon**	***Vietnamese chili paste***
	1	**teaspoon**	***sesame oil***
Mix together just until hot.			

175 North Center
Jackson
733-6803

Louie's Steak and Seafood has as its home an older log house built in 1935, originally a family homestead where resident, Gilbert "Boots" Nelson was born in the upstairs bedroom, now a dining room!

Purchasing the building in 1986, Terry and Stella Travis have created a fine restaurant offering a diverse menu which features the freshest ingredients available. They are proud to be the home of the Wyoming Wellington, a signature entree offered along with seafood, pasta and chicken entrees.

Terry and Stella have given us two very different menus with accompanying recipes; one with four courses that are sure to satisfy even the most ravenous of appetities, and another that is perfect for light summer fare. They hope you will enjoy the cookbook and will please come by and say hello. . . "Louie - this could be the beginning of a beautiful friendship!"

MENU FOR FOUR

Shrimp Marinette

Cucumber Tomato Salad
with Green Onion Dijon Vinaigrette

Grilled Swordfish
with Fresh Basil Dill Sauce

Parsleyed Red Potatoes

Chocolate Mocha Pudding

Chef Terry Travis

SHRIMP MARINETTE

Serves 4

In blender or food processor, combine until smooth. . .	4		***artichoke hearts***
(batter)	2	**large**	***egg yolks***
	3	**ounces**	***dijon mustard***

Into batter, dip. . .	8	**jumbo**	***shrimp,*** peeled and deveined
Coat shrimp with. . .	$1^1/_2$	**cups**	***bread crumbs***

In skillet, heat. . .	2	**cups**	***olive oil***

Add shrimp and cook over medium high heat for 2-1/2 minutes on each side until lightly golden brown.

Serve immediately with. . . ***cocktail sauce***

CUCUMBER TOMATO SALAD WITH GREEN ONION DIJON VINAIGRETTE

Serves 4

Wash, drain well and tear into small pieces...	**6**	**leaves**	***romaine***
	6	**leaves**	***green leaf***

In bowl, combine...	**1**	**cup**	***cucumber,*** peeled and chopped
	1	**cup**	***tomatoes,*** seeded and chopped
	$^1/_3$	**cup**	***red onion,*** chopped

On chilled salad plates, place a mixture of the *romaine* and *green leaf* lettuce. Place a mound of the tomato and cucumber mixture in the center, and drizzle liberally with **Green Onion Dijon Vinaigrette.**

Green Onion Dijon Vinaigrette

In food processor, combine...	**1**	**cup**	***red wine vinegar***
	$^1/_4$	**cup**	***dijon mustard***
	2	**tablespoons**	***green onion,*** chopped
	1	**clove**	***garlic,*** crushed
	$^1/_2$	**teaspoon**	***black pepper***

With processor running, slowly add...	**$1^1/_2$**	**cups**	***olive oil***

Cover and refrigerate until ready to use.

GRILLED SWORDFISH WITH FRESH BASIL DILL SAUCE

Serves 4

*It's important to use **fresh** swordfish with this delicate marinade.*

For this recipe, you will need...	4	**6 ounce**	***swordfish steaks***
In shallow pan, combine... (*marinade*)	1	**cup**	***olive oil***
	$1/4$	**cup**	***lemon juice***
	$1/4$	**cup**	***fresh basil,*** chopped
	2	**tablespoons**	***fresh dill,*** chopped
	2	**tablespoons**	***green onions,*** finely chopped

Marinate swordfish in mixture for 30 minutes. Reserve marinade.

Grill swordfish on barbeque, about 3 minutes each side. Don't overcook! While swordfish is cooking, prepare the **Fresh Basil Dill Sauce**.

Fresh Basil Dill Sauce

In saucepan, over medium high heat, saute until transparent...	2	**tablespoons**	***olive oil***
	1	**large**	***garlic clove,*** minced
	1	**large**	***shallot,*** minced
Add and reduce by half...	$1/2$	**cup**	***white wine***
Add and cook 2 minutes...	2	**medium**	***tomatoes,*** seeded and chopped
Add and cook over **high heat** 1 minute...			***reserved marinade***
Remove from heat and swirl in...	8	**tablespoons**	***butter,*** cubed

Serve immediately over swordfish.

PARSLEYED RED POTATOES

Serves 4

In saucepan, boil until half done. . .	8	small	***red potatoes,*** sliced 3/4" thick
Drain potatoes well.			

In large saute pan, over medium high heat, combine . . .			***potatoes***
	$^1/_4$	cup	***olive oil***
	3	tablespoons	***parsley,*** finely chopped

Cook about 5 minutes, or until potatoes are light brown.

CHOCOLATE MOCHA PUDDING

Serves 4

In saucepan, melt together, stirring regularly. . .	2	ounces	***butter***
	4	ounces	***semi-sweet chocolate,*** chopped
	$^1/_4$	teaspoon	***instant coffee crystals***

Don't let it get too hot — take it off the heat as soon as it is melted and beat until smooth and glossy. Let stand 2 minutes to cool slightly.

In separate bowls, place. . .	1	cup	***heavy cream***
	2		***egg yolks***

To each bowl, add and whip until fluffy. . .	1	tablespoon	***sugar***

Fold egg yolk mixture into chocolate, blending it well. Next fold in the whipped cream. Pour into dessert dishes and chill until ready to serve.

MENU FOR SIX

Stuffed Seafood Shells Marinara

Zucchini Saute

Strawberries and Peaches with Yogurt Cream

Chef Terry Travis

STUFFED SEAFOOD SHELLS MARINARA

Serves 6

This rich pasta dish makes a wonderful supper when served with a fresh vegetable and a good bottle of chianti.

In boiling water, cook just until al dente. . .	**30**	**large**	***macaroni shells***
Rinse well with cold water and drain. Set aside.			
In large skillet, saute 2-3 minutes. . .	**1**	**pound**	***shrimp,*** medium size
There should still be a slight opaqueness along the spine. Chop coarsely and set aside.			
Next, saute 2-3 minutes. . .	**1**	**pound**	***scallops,*** large
There should still be a slight opaqueness in the center of each scallop. Chop coarsely and set aside.			
In bowl, beat until smooth and fluffy. . .	$^1/_2$	**pound**	***cream cheese***
Add and mix well. . .	$^1/_2$	**pound**	***ricotta cheese***
	$^1/_2$	**pound**	***mozzarella cheese,*** shredded
			reserved shrimp
			reserved scallops

Stuff shells with seafood mixture and bake in shallow baking pan, covered, in a **preheated** 450° oven for 15-20 minutes; just until hot. Serve immediately draped with **Marinara Sauce.**

Marinara Sauce

In medium hot skillet, combine. . .	2	tablespoons	*olive oil*
	3	large	*garlic cloves,* minced
	2	large	*shallots,* minced
Saute until shallots are clear.			

Add and cook 2 minutes. . .	1/2	pound	*mushrooms,* thinly sliced

---

Add and cook to reduce liquid by half. . .	2	cups	*white wine*
then add. . .	3	medium	*plum tomatoes,* seeded and chopped
	6	whole	*green onions,* chopped

Cook for two more minutes.

ZUCCHINI SAUTE

Serves 6

In medium hot skillet, saute for 30 seconds. . .	1	tablespoons	*olive oil*
	1	large	*garlic clove,* minced
	1	large	*shallot,* minced

Add and saute for 2-3 minutes. . .	1	tablespoons	*olive oil*
	6	medium	*zucchini,* cut into strips
Zucchini should be crunchy!			
Sprinkle liberally with. . .	1/2 - 3/4	cup	*parmesan cheese,* freshly grated

Toss and serve.

STRAWBERRIES AND PEACHES WITH YOGURT CREAM

Serves 6

An easy and quick, light dessert suitable any time, especially after heavy meals.

Peel and slice...	**3**		***peaches***
Combine with...	**24**		***strawberries,*** washed and hulled.

In separate bowl, gently fold together...	**1**	**cup**	***heavy cream,*** whipped
	1	**cup**	***plain yogurt***

Keep fruit and yogurt cream chilled until ready to use. To serve, drape fruit with cream.

Teton Village
733-4913

The Mangy Moose began in 1967 as a spaghetti emporium. It has grown over the years to become one of the area's most popular restaurants and saloon. Owners Pat Mahin and Jim Terry, in their insatiable quest for antiques and unusual memorabilia, have created one of the most unique dining rooms in the Rocky Mountains. Their search for new and unusual foods introduced Jackson Hole to its first salad bar, as well as many ethnic dishes such as Mexican Fajitas and the Valley's first oriental food.

The saloon was the first in the area to introduce its own brand of lager beer, known as Moose Brew. Shows from comedy acts to performers such as Dave Mason, Nicolette Larson, Leon Russel and the Ozark Moutain Daredevils are regular events in the saloon.

In addition to fine food and entertainment, the Mangy Moose houses a variety of unique shops offering everything from antiques and Jackson Hole souveniers to a full package liquor store.

Pat and Jim's philosophy of offering hearty portions of quality food and spirits at affordable prices in an incredible atmosphere has made the Mangy Moose a must for Jackson Hole visitors, and a tradition for locals.

MENU FOR EIGHT

New Orleans Style Barbeque Shrimp

Garden Salad with Mangy Moose Blue Cheese Dressing

Whiskey Steak

Baked Idaho Spuds

Fresh Corn on the Cob

Peanut Butter Pie

Chef Bill Paju

NEW ORLEANS STYLE BARBEQUE SHRIMP

Serves 4

This Cajun recipe has been a favorite appetizer at the Moose for years. It also makes a great main course. Scallops, squid, crawfish or any combination of shellfish work well with this recipe. We recommend serving it with lots of lemon, fresh bread for dipping and a frosty mug of beer — Moose Brew beer, of course!

In small bowl, blend together *(cajun spice mix)...*	1	**teaspoon**	***paprika***
	1	**teaspoon**	***cayenne pepper***
	1	**teaspoon**	***black pepper***
	1/2	**teaspoon**	***crushed red chilis***
	1/2	**teaspoon**	***onion salt***
	1/2	**teaspoon**	***oregano***
	1/2	**teaspoon**	***thyme***
Set aside.			

Peel and devein...	1	**pound**	***shrimp,*** medium to large

In large skillet, heat...	1/4	**pound**	***unsalted butter***
	1	**tablespoon**	***fresh garlic,*** minced
Add and saute over medium heat...			***cajun spice mix***
			shrimp
Saute shrimp 1-2 minutes per side (they should still be slightly opaque down the middle of their spine).			
Add and simmer briefly, just until opaqueness is gone...	1	**dash**	***worcestershire sauce***
	1/4	**cup**	***beer***

Serve.

GARDEN SALAD WITH MANGY MOOSE BLUE CHEESE DRESSING

1 Quart

As a dressing over any combination of crisp greens and salad toppings, or as a dip with fresh vegetables, this unique and spicy blue cheese dressing has as its base, zesty Italian seasonings. This is our own recipe for blue cheese dressing which is served at the Mangy Moose salad bar.

Using electric mixer on low, or by hand, blend together in this order...

1/2	**cup**	***salad oil***
1/2	**cup**	***red wine vinegar***
1	**tablespoon**	***lemon juice***
1 1/2	**teaspoons**	***black pepper***
1 1/2	**teaspoons**	***crushed red chilis***
1 1/2	**teaspoons**	***garlic,*** granulated
1 1/2	**teaspoons**	***oregano***
1 1/2	**teaspoons**	***onion salt***
1/2	**cup**	***mayonnaise***
1/2	**cup**	***buttermilk***
1	**cup**	***sour cream***
1/2	**pound**	***blue cheese,*** crumbled

WHISKEY STEAK

Serves 4

The Mangy Moose uses this marinade on top sirloin steak, but any cut of beef, chicken, ribs or even fresh seafood can be used. Cooked over hot coals on your BBQ is the best. Served with piping hot ears of corn and baked potatoes, you have yourself a summer feast to enjoy.

For this recipe, you will need...	**2-3**	**pounds**	***your favorite beef steak***

In bowl, blend together...	**8**	**ounces**	***barbeque sauce***
(marinade)	**1/2**	**cup**	***teriyaki sauce***
	1/2	**cup**	***pineapple juice***
	1/2	**cup**	***dijon mustard***
	1/4	**cup**	***salad oil***
	1/4	**cup**	***whiskey or bourbon***
	1	**small**	***onion,*** finely diced
	1 1/2	**tablespoons**	***fresh garlic,*** minced

Use this marinade to cover the meat of your choice for 4 to 24 hours (the longer, the better) before broiling or grilling to desired doneness.

PEANUT BUTTER PIE

This is a long-standing favorite dessert of Jackson Hole locals. For delicious variations, try topping a slice with warm honey or hot fudge and, of course, plenty of fresh whipped cream.

To make crust, mix together. . .	2	**cups**	***chocolate cookie crumbs,*** well crushed
	1/4	**cup**	***sugar***
	1/4	**pound**	***unsalted butter,*** melted

Press mixture into bottom and sides of 9" pie pan. Let set in freezer while preparing filling.

Using electric mixer, beat until stiff. . .	1	**cup**	***heavy cream***
Blend in until smooth. . .	8	**ounces**	***cream cheese,*** softened, at room temperature

---

Add and mix well. . .	1	**cup**	***peanut butter***
	1	**14 -ounce can**	***sweetened condensed milk***
	1	**teaspoon**	***vanilla extract***
	1	**teaspoon**	***lemon juice***

Pour mixture into crust and freeze. Allow to soften slightly at room temperature before serving.

5600 West Highway 22
Wilson
733-8288

In a large, rustic log cabin which originally housed a general store and post office, Nora's Fish Creek Inn opened its doors in 1982. Nora's quickly became a favorite spot where locals meet for breakfast. The warm and rustic atmosphere, together with such dishes as Huevos Rancheros with green chile salsa and the breakfast burrito are responsible for such success.

Many of Nora's regular customers have been there from the beginning, as well as most of her staff. Nora's patrons, resident or visitor, always feel at home and enjoy good home cooking with homemade sauces and fresh baked goods in a friendly, bustling environment.

In the last couple of years, the Fish Creek Inn has expanded to serve dinner in the evening, offering a small but varied menu featuring Mexican food along with seafood, chicken and steaks. For their part in this book, one of the recipes Nora is sharing with us is her famous green salsa recipe; a well-kept secret until now!

FAVORITE BREAKFAST ENTREES

Huevos Rancheros with Nora's Green Salsa

and Refried Beans

Blueberry Pancakes

Biscuits & Gravy

Nora Tygum

HUEVOS RANCHEROS WITH NORA'S GREEN SALSA

Serves 4

Nora's is famous for her Huevos Rancheros. Every day of the week, and especially on Saturdays and Sundays, customers crowd her restaurant for breakfast. Many of them order this dish time after time.

For this recipe, you will need...			
	4		***corn tortillas,*** fried
	8	**large**	***eggs,*** fried or scrambled
	1	**pound**	***mozzarella cheese (or) jack cheese,*** shredded
	4	**cups**	***refried beans***

To serve, place a fried *corn tortilla* on each plate; spreadthe tortilla with a scoop of **Refried Beans**. Place two *eggs* on top of the beans, followed by a ladleful of **Nora's Green Sauce**. Top it all off with a healthy handful of shredded *mozzarella cheese*. Place under a broiler just until bubbly. Watch closely so it won't burn!

Nora's Green Sauce

In large saucepan or stockpot, saute until onions are translucent...			
	$^1/_4$	**pound**	***margarine,*** melted
	$2^1/_2$	**cups**	***onions,*** chopped

Add and simmer 20 minutes...	12	**cups**	***chicken stock***
	1	**27 ounce can**	***diced green chiles***
	$1^1/_2$	**teaspoons**	***cumin***
	$1^1/_2$	**teaspoons**	***leaf oregano***
	1	**teaspoon**	***white pepper***
	1	**teaspoon**	***crushed red chiles***

Thicken with...	$^1/_2$	**cup**	***flour***
	$^1/_4$	**cup**	***cornstarch***

Keep warm to serve immediately. For use later, allow to cool to room temperature, cover, and store in the refrigerator.

REFRIED BEANS

About 1 Quart

Canned refried beans can, of course, be used in Nora's Heuvos Rancheros. But try making your own for a new treat! Cooking beans long enough — until very soft — is the secret to removing the gassy side effects.

In large saucepan, combine and bring to a boil. . .

	8	cups	*water*
	$1^1/_2$	pounds	*dried pinto beans*

Boil beans about 3-4 hours, adding water as needed, until beans are soft enough to mash *easily* with your fingers. Drain water from beans to just below the top of the beans; then mash them.

Place saucepan with mashed beans over low heat, and add. . .

	$^1/_2$	pound	*margarine*
	2	tablespoons	*salt*
	1	tablespoon	*white pepper*
	1	tablespoon	*cumin*
	$^1/_2$	teaspoon	*garlic powder*

Stir well to thoroughly blend spices and margarine into the beans.

BLUEBERRY PANCAKES

Makes 8 Large Pancakes

Pancakes at Nora's are large and fluffy, and a big favorite with her customers. To keep up with the demand, a large batch of "dry mix" ingredients is kept on hand to be portioned out and mixed with the liquid ingredients to make their pancake batter on a daily basis. Here is a 'slightly' scaled down recipe for Nora's pancakes.

To make **dry mix**, blend together...	**$1\frac{1}{2}$**	**pounds**	***flour***
	5	**tablespoons**	***baking powder***
	2	**tablespoons**	***sugar***
	$\frac{1}{4}$	**teaspoon**	***salt***

When you are ready to mix your batter, combine and beat well...	**2**	**cups**	***milk***
	2	**large**	***eggs***
	3	**tablespoons**	***vegetable oil***

Stir in...	**2**	**cups**	***dry mix***

Mix batther only until dry ingredients are moistened. Batter should be lumpy.

To complete this recipe, you will need...	**2-3**	**cups**	***blueberries***

Bake pancakes on a hot griddle or skillet. Just before flipping the pancakes to the other side (when top side is bubbly), sprinkle the top of each cake with blueberries. Turn and brown the other sides.

BISCUITS AND GRAVY

Makes 1 Dozen

Old fashioned and hearty, this breakfast will stick with you all day!

In bowl, thoroughly blend together. . .	$2^1/_2$	**cups**	***flour***
	3	**teaspoons**	***baking powder***
	$1^1/_2$	**teaspoons**	***sugar***
	1	**teaspoon**	***salt***
	$^1/_2$	**teaspoon**	***cream of tarter***

With a pastry blender, cut in. . .	5	**tablespoons**	***crisco***

Mixture should be crumbly but will stick together if squeezed by hand.

Make a well in center of mixture and pour in. . .	$^3/_4$	**cup**	***milk***

Stir to combine until dough starts pulling away from sides of the bowl and sticking together. Turn dough out onto a floured surface and knead gently for about half a minute. On a clean floured surface, roll dough out to a thickness of about half an inch, using a rolling pin or the palm of your hand. Cut dough in rounds using a cutter with its edge floured (be sure not to twist cutter), place on ungreased baking sheets, brush tops with milk and bake in a **preheated** 450° oven for 15 to 17 minutes. Serve with **Gravy.**

Gravy

In skillet, saute until browned. . .	6	**ounces**	***Jimmy Dean sausage,*** crumbled

Set aside.

In another skillet, combine to form roux. . .	$^{1}/_{4}$	**pound**	*margarine*
	$^{1}/_{2}$	**heaping cup**	*flour*

Cook over medium heat, stirring constantly, until walnut brown in color.

Add, stirring constantly. . .	**$1^{1}/_{2}$**	**quarts**	*half and half*
	$1^{1}/_{2}$	**teaspoons**	*salt*
	$^{3}/_{4}$	**teaspoon**	*white pepper*
then add. . .			*crumbled sausage*

Stir constantly and cook until hot. **Don't allow to boil.**

30 South King
Jackson
733-9777

In the summer of 1986 Off Broadway opened its doors featuring a classy yet casual atmosphere, an open kitchen, two intimate dining rooms and a private banquet room with balcony. Located in the heart of downtown Jackson, just off the town square, Off Broadway boasts a large deck for summer dining, always a delight with its array of flowers and bright blue umbrellas.

The success of Off Broadway is due to the close attention paid to the high quality of ingredients selected, creative menus, and in the consistency it has maintained in preparing and presenting fine cuisine. Off Broadway chefs focus on lighter fare, creating imaginative foods for healthy appetites.

Changing with the seasons, their menu offers a variety of traditional and inventive recipes. On any given night, entrees may be complemented by sauces such as Italian pesto, French beurre blanc, Thai peanut sauce, or Mexican roasted chili salsa. Known primarily for grilled seafoods and a variety of fresh pastas, Off Broadway also serves a selection of choice meats, poultry and wild game.

Open for dinner year around, and lunch and dinner in summers, Off Broadway also offers private catering. Complementing its food is a wide selection of fine wines, cocktails, gourmet coffees and espresso. Its "Home Collection," features gourmet selections packaged for the comfort of dining at home and for unique gifts.

As illustration of their wonderfully diverse menu, Off Broadway has given us two very different menus with accompanying recipes.

MENU FOR FOUR

"A TASTE OF THE FAR EAST"

Chicken and Coconut Milk Soup

Thai Beef Salad

Grilled Chicken
with Peanut Sauce

Shrimp and Scallops
with Thai Sauce

Chef Alan Belliveau

CHICKEN AND COCONUT MILK SOUP (GAENG DOM YAM GAI)

Serves 4

In large saucepan, combine and simmer for 2 hours. . .	**5**	**cups**	***chicken stock****
	1	**stalk**	***fresh lemon grass****
	2	**ounces**	***fresh ginger,*** sliced
	2	**cloves**	***garlic,*** whole
Strain broth and return to heat. (Or broth can be made to this point 2 days ahead of time and stored in the refrigerator.			

With broth simmering, add. . .	**10**	**ounces**	***coconut milk,*** canned
Bring back up to heat.			

Add and simmer for another 3 minutes. . .	**8**	**ounces**	***boneless chicken breast,*** cut into bite size pieces

Finally, add. . .	**2**	**whole**	***limes,*** juice of
	3	**tablespoons**	***fish sauce****
	$^1/_2$	**cup**	***green onion,*** sliced
	2	**tablespoons**	***cilantro,*** coarsely chopped

Serve immediately.

**Homemade is best (see recipe on page 258), or good quality canned.*

***Available in specialty food stores or through mial order spice merchants (see page iv).*

THAI BEEF SALAD (YAM NEUA)

Serves 4

On barbeque or grill, cook until rare. . .	1/2	**pound**	*lean beef*
Chill beef, then thinly slice it diagonally.			
Wash, drain well and tear into bite-size pieces. . .	**1**	**head**	*bibb lettuce*
Coarsely chop. . .	**8**		*mint leaves*
	8		*cilantro leaves*
Slice to thin rings. . .	**1**	**small**	*red onion*

Arrange lettuce on salad plates and sprinkle with mint and cilantro. Lay beef slices over lettuce followed by rings of red onion. Drizzle with **Yam Neua Dressing**.

Yam Neua Dressing

In container, combine. . .	**2**	**tablespoons**	*fresh lime juice*
	1	**tablespoon**	*fish sauce*
	5	**cloves**	*garlic,* minced
	3	**whole**	*jalapeno peppers,* finely diced
	2	**teaspoons**	*sugar*
	1	**teaspoon**	*crushed red pepper flakes*

Shake well and serve.

GRILLED CHICKEN WITH PEANUT SAUCE (GAI TUA)

Serves 4

In bowl, combine. . . (*marinade*)	$^1/_4$	**cup**	***olive oil***
	4	**tablespoons**	***sesame oil***
	2	**tablespoons**	***soy sauce***
	2	**ounces**	***fresh ginger,*** chopped
	2	**ounces**	***garlic,*** chopped

Cut into strips and marinate for 6 to 8 hours. . .	**12**	**ounces**	***chicken breast,*** boneless and skinless

Soak in warm (not hot) water for 15-20 minutes, until soft. . .	**12**	**ounces**	***cellophane noodles***

Don't leave noodles in water too long, they will get mushy. Drain well.

For garnish, slice. . .	**2**	**whole**	***green onions***

Cook chicken strips over hot coals or grill over open flame on both sides for 2-3 minutes. Place chicken on cellophane noodles and top with **Peanut Sauce** and green onions.

Peanut Sauce

In saucepan, combine and bring to a boil. . .	4	**cups**	***coconut milk***
	2	**cups**	***crunchy peanut butter***
	1	**large**	***onion,*** finely diced
	$^1/_4$	**cup**	***fish sauce***
	$^1/_4$	**cup**	***soy sauce***
	$^1/_4$	**cup**	***brown sugar***
	1	**teaspoon**	***cayenne pepper***

Simmer briefly then set aside until ready to use. Sauce can be refrigerated for up to 1 week.

SHRIMP AND SCALLOPS WITH THAI SAUCE (NAM PRIK)

Serves 4

Soak in warm (not hot) water for 15-20 minutes, until soft. . .	**12**	**ounces**	***cellophane noodles***
Don't leave noodles water too long, they will get mushy. Drain well.			
For garnish, slice and set aside. . .	**2**	**whole**	***green onions***
In baking dish, place. . .	**1**	**pound**	***shrimp,*** medium size, peeled and deveined
	1	**pound**	***scallops***

Pour **Thai Sauce** over seafood and bake, covered, in a **preheated** 350° oven for approximately 15-20 minutes, until shrimp is cooked. Serve over cellophane noodles and garnish with green onions.

Thai Sauce

Combine and mix well. . .	**1**	**cup**	***olive oil***
	3/4	**cup**	***rice vinegar***
	3	**tablespoons**	***fish sauce***
	2	**tablespoons**	***chile oil***
	1/4	**cup**	***fresh cilantro,*** chopped
	1/4	**cup**	***fresh mint,*** chopped
	1	**teaspoon**	***fresh ginger,*** minced
	2	**cloves**	***garlic,*** minced
	1	**whole**	***lemon,*** zest of

MENU FOR FOUR

Hungarian Mushroom Soup

Spinach Salad
with Sweet Vinaigrette

Pasta Puttanesca

Decadent Chocolate Cake

Chef Suzanne Zowarka

HUNGARIAN MUSHROOM SOUP

Serves 4

In large stockpot, combine over medium heat. . .	1/2	cup	***butter,*** melted
	1	cup	***white onion,*** minced
	1	tablespoon	***Hungarian paprika***
	1	tablespoon	***fresh dill*** (1 teaspoon dried)
	1	tablespoon	***worcestershire sauce***
	2	teaspoons	***white pepper***
Cook, stirring occasionally, until onions are transparent.			
Add and cook for 5 minutes. . .	1	pound	***mushrooms,*** sliced

---

Stir in and cook for another 5 minutes, stirring often. . .	1/4	cup	***flour***

Slowly stir in. . .	3	cups	***chicken stock****
	1	cup	***half and half (or) heavy cream***

Cook over low heat for 15-20 minutes.

**Homemade is best (see recipe on page 258), or good quality canned.*

SPINACH SALAD WITH SWEET VINAIGRETTE

Serves 4

Wash, trim stems and drain well. . .	1/2	**pound**	***fresh spinach***

Store in cloth or plastic bag in refrigerator to chill.

In skillet, fry until crisp. . .	4	**slices**	***bacon***

Drain bacon well and crumble.

To complete this recipe, you will need. . .	1/4	**pound**	***baby shrimp,*** cooked
	1	**medium**	***tomato,*** cut into wedges
	1	**cup**	***croutons***
	1/4	**cup**	***parmesan cheese,*** freshly grated

Place equal portions of spinach on chilled salad plates and top with bacon, *shrimp, tomato wedges, croutons* and *parmesan cheese.* Drizzle with **Sweet Vinaigrette.**

Sweet Vinaigrette

In food processor, puree. . .	1/4	**small**	***onion***

Add andprocess until smooth. . .	3/4	**cup**	***red wine vinegar***
	1/3	**cup**	***ketchup***
	2	**tablespoons**	***worcestershire sauce***
	1	**tablespoon**	***sugar***

With processor running, slowly add. . .	1	**cup**	***vegetable oil***

Store in covered contained in refrigerator for up to 1 week.

PASTA PUTTANESCA

Serves 4

In saute pan over medium heat, combine...	**7**	**tablespoons**	***olive oil***
	2	**cloves**	***garlic,*** minced
	4	**ounces**	***anchovies,*** minced
Saute for 5 minutes.			

Stir in...	**3**	**medium**	***tomatoes,*** diced
	4	**ounces**	***black olives,*** sliced
	2	**tablespoons**	***capers***
Simmer for 20 minutes, stirring occasionally.			

While sauce is simmering, cook until al dente...	**14**	**ounces**	***pasta of choice***
Drain well.			

To complete this recipe, you will need...	**2**	**tablespoons**	***parmesan cheese,*** freshly grated
	2	**tablespoons**	***fresh parsley,*** chopped

Add pasta to sauce, toss well and cook briefly to heat pasta. To serve, sprinkle with *parmesan cheese* and *parsley*.

DECADENT CHOCOLATE CAKE

9" Cake

In top of double boiler, combine. . .	1	**cup**	***unsalted butter***
	7	**ounces**	***semi-sweet chocolate,*** chopped
	2	**ounces**	***unsweet. chocolate,*** chopped
Melt over simmering water, stirring until smooth. Let cool.			

In large bowl, whisk together until well blended . .	4	**large**	***eggs***
	$1^1/_2$	**cups**	***sugar***

Whisk in. . .	1	**tablespoon**	***flour***
followed by. . .			***chocolate mixture***

To complete this recipe, you will need. . .	3	**tablespoons**	***sugar***
	1	**cup**	***heavy cream,*** whipped

Butter 9" springform pan and sprinkle bottom and sides with *sugar*. Wrap pan with foil around bottom and up sides.

Pour batter into pan and place in large baking pan. Pour enough water into baking pan to come 1/2" up side of springform pan. Bake in **preheated** 325° for about 1 hour, until cake is firm and pick inserted in the center comes out moist with crumbs attached.

Remove cake from water bath, remove foil wrapping and cool completely. To serve, spoon **Raspberry Sauce** on dessert plate, place wedge of cake on sauce and top off with a dollop of *whipped cream*.

Raspberry Sauce

In bowl, combine. . .	**1**	**pint**	***fresh raspberries (or) 1 package frozen***
	1-2	**tablespoons**	***sugar***

Let stand for 10 minutes to dissolve sugar and release berry juices. Puree in blender or food processor. Strain to remove seeds (optional).

Stir in. . .	**1**	**teaspoon**	***fresh lemon juice***

Note: Any type of berries will make an excellent sauce for this cake. Some berries may need less sugar.

Snow King Resort
Jackson
733-5200

Rafferty's, with it's high, beamed ceiling and unbeatable view of the town of Jackson, is located in the Snow King Resort, a 204 room full-service hotel located at the base of the Snow King Mountain. Getting its name from Neil Rafferty, one of the original founders of Snow King Ski Area in 1939, Rafferty's specializes in its extraordinary Sunday champagne brunch.

Adjacent to Rafferty's is the Atrium Restaurant, with its view of Snow King Mountain. In addition to serving lunch and dinner with a wide array of salads, sandwiches, main-course entrees, fresh baked breads and desserts, a specialty of the Atrium is its elaborate breakfast buffet served daily in the open, plant-filled mezzanine of the Snow King. The Atrium has become a favorite escape for locals and visitors alike, from the hustle and bustle of town.

MENU FOR SIX

Salmon Roulade with Broiled Leeks

Mushroom Broccoli Soup

Marinated Cantaloupe
in Zinfandel Coriander Dressing

Rocky Mountain Lamb Chops
with Sauce Charcutiere

Grilled Melons and Peppers
with Prosciutto and Fresh Mint

Italian (Biga) Bread

Shortbread with Fresh Strawberries

SALMON ROULADE WITH BROILED LEEKS

Serves 6

In a very hot skillet, heat. . .	**2**	**tablespoons**	***olive oil***
Add and saute until just barely soft. . .	**1**	**bunch**	***fresh spinach,*** washed and drained

---

In food processor, pulse together, until well mixed. . .			***cooked spinach***
	1	**ounce**	***fresh dill***
	1	**large**	***egg***
	2	**ounces**	***feta cheese***
	1	**ounce**	***cream cheese***

To complete this recipe, you will need. . .	**1**	**pound**	***salmon filet,*** bones and skin removed
Slice diagonally across grain into 1/4″ x 1″ x 4" strips.			
And also. . .	**4**		***leeks,*** white part only
Split down center and wash gently so as not to separate individual leaves.			

Lay each *salmon strip* flat and place a small amount (about 1/2 teaspoon) of spinach/cheese mixture on one end. Starting with that end, roll up each strip of salmon and place it on a lightly oiled baking sheet. Bake in a **preheated** 375° oven for 5 minutes. Cool to room temperature before chilling in refrigerator.

While roulades are chilling; slice white part of *leeks* at an angle into diamond-shaped segments, drizzle with olive oil and broil 2-3 minutes or until corners begin to brown and curl. Allow to cool.

To serve, arrange leeks and salmon roulades on individual plates.

MUSHROOM BROCCOLI SOUP

Serves 6

In large saucepan, over medium heat, combine. . .	**3**	**tablespoons**	***olive oil***
	1	**pound**	***mushrooms,*** sliced
	2	**medium**	***red bell pepper,*** julienne
	1	**medium**	***onion,*** diced
	3	**cloves**	***garlic,*** minced
Saute until onions are transparent.			

Add and bring to a boil. . .	**4**	**cups**	***chicken stock****
	2	**tablespoons**	***capers,*** with juice
	1	**whole**	***lemon,*** juice of
	1	**sprig**	***fresh tarragon,*** leaves stripped off whole
	1	**sprig**	***fresh thyme,*** chopped
	1/4	**teaspoon**	***turmeric***
Reduce to a simmer for 30 minutes.			

Increase heat to high and add. . .	**2**	**tablespoons**	***roux*****
Whisk to break up lumps. Simmer 5 minutes and add. . .			***salt and pepper to taste***

To complete this recipe, you will need. . .	**1**	**head**	***broccoli,*** broken into florets

Just before serving the soup, steam the *broccoli* flowerets until they are bright green in color. Add broccoli florets to each serving of soup.

**Homemade is best (see recipe on page 258), or good quality canned.*

***To make **roux**, melt 4 tablespoons butter in small pan and stir in 1/4 heaping cup of flour. Stir and cook over medium high heat until golden in color.*

MARINATED CANTALOUPE WITH ZINFANDEL CORIANDER DRESSSING

Serves 6

For optimum flavor, the cantaloupe must be marinated the day before serving, and the coriander dressing should be made just before serving and served at room temperature.

The **day before**, peel and cut into wedges. . .	**2**	**medium**	***cantaloupe***

In bowl, combine. . .	**1**	**bottle**	***zinfandel wine***
	1	**cup**	***sugar***

Stir until sugar is dissolved.

Place cantaloupe wedges in a small baking pan and pour wine marinade over, making sure all wedges are at least half covered with marinade. Cover and refrigerate for 12-24 hours.

To serve, arrange 5-6 wedges of cantaloupe on a pool of freshly made **Coriander Dressing** and garnish each plate with fresh *cilantro leaves**.

Coriander Dressing

In food processor, blend. . .	**1/4**	**cup**	***dry sherry***
	1/2	**cup**	***sugar***
	1	**large**	***egg***
	1	**tablespoon**	***lemon juice***
	2	**teaspoons**	***coriander seed***
	1	**teaspoon**	***Hungarian paprika***
	1/4	**teaspoon**	***salt***

With processor running, slowly add. . .	**1**	**cup**	***olive oil***

Pour dressing into a bowl and fold in. . .	**1**	**bunch**	***fresh cilantro*,*** leaves only, chopped

(*save whole leaves for garnish)

ROCKY MOUNTAIN LAMB CHOPS WITH SAUCE CHARCUTIERE

Serves 6

For this sauce, the better the wine you use, the better the sauce! Homemade brown sauce or beef gravy is best, but canned brown sauce can be used instead.

For this recipe, you will need. . .	**18**		***lamb rib chops***

Have your butcher trim them so the bone are completely clean up to the chop. Brush *lamb ribs* with olive oil and broil on a charcoal or gas grill to required doneness (4 minutes per side for medium).

Serve with **Sauce Charcutiere**.

Sauce Charcutiere

In large saucepan, over medium heat, combine. . .	**2**	**cups**	***brown sauce****
	1	**cup**	***beef stock***
	1/2	**cup**	***red wine***
	1/2	**cup**	***dry sherry***
	1/4	**cup**	***red wine vinegar***
Reduce by half, stirring occasionally.			

In a skillet, saute until golden brown. . .	**1**	**tablespoon**	***unsalted butter***
	1	**medium**	***onion,*** diced

To reduced sauce, add. . .			***sauteed onion***
	1/3	**cup**	***gherkin pickles,*** diced
	1/4	**teaspoon**	***black pepper***
	1/4	**teaspoon**	***nutmeg***
	1/8	**teaspoon**	***ground clove***

Simmer for 20-30 minutes to blend flavors.

**Homemade is best (see recipe on page 260), or a good beef gravy.*

GRILLED MELONS AND PEPPERS WITH PROSCIUTTO AND FRESH MINT

Serves 6

This recipe works best on a charcoal or gas grill, but it can be done in a dry cast-iron skillet over medium high heat if the pan is preheated well. The flavor will be similar, only the stripes of the grill will be missing.

Seed and cut into thin wedges...	**1**	**whole**	***cantaloupe melon***
	1	**whole**	***honeydew melon***
Seed and cut into 1/2" strips...	**1**	**medium**	***green bell pepper***
	1	**medium**	***red bell pepper***
	1	**medium**	***yellow bell pepper***
Cut into fine julienne...	**2**	**ounces**	***prosciutto***
To complete this recipe, you will need...	**1/2**	**cup**	***olive oil***
	2	**ounces**	***fresh mint leaves***

Brush melon wedges and pepper strips with *olive oil* and grill for 1-2 minutes on each side. Toss melon and peppers with prosciutto and *fresh mint leaves*. Serve.

ITALIAN (BIGA) BREAD

Makes 2 Loaves

This is a wonderful 'sponge' bread with a crisp crust. Don't decide to make it at the last minute. The yeast mixture must be made the day before you make the dough, and the dough itself must rise three times for the best flavor and texture.

In a medium-size **glass** or **plastic** bowl, mix together... *(biga)*	1/2	**cup**	***white flour***
	1/4	**teaspoon**	***dry active yeast***
	1/8	**teaspoon**	***salt*** (uniodized)
	1/2	**cup**	***distilled water*** (no chlorine)
Cover and let sit in a cool (not cold) place overnight.			

In the morning, add to the biga and mix well...	**1**	**cup**	***distilled water***
	1	**tablespoon**	***salt*** (uniodized)

Add 1 cup at a time, stirring after each addition, to make a soft dough...	**6**	**cups**	***flour***
Amount of flour is approximate. Allow dough to sit, covered with a damp cloth, for 10 minutes.			

On a cool, very lightly floured surface, knead dough for 10 minutes or until it is smooth and silky, not sticky. Place dough in a cool place (60°-70° at most), cover with a damp cloth and allow to rise until doubled in bulk, about 2 to 2-1/2 hours. Punch down and allow to rise again until doubled in bulk, about 1-1/2 to 2 hours.

Divide dough into 4 pieces and form each into a ball. Flour each ball well, place on well-floured baking sheet. Allow to rise in a cool place, covered with a damp cloth, until doubled in bulk.

Slash the top of each loaf with a sharp knife or razor blade and bake in a **preheated** 425° oven for 20-25 minutes, until dark golden brown. It is important that the temperature at which you bake these loaves is an accurate 425°. Too low a temperature will produce a crust that is tough rather than crisp, and too hot an oven will burn the crust before the bread is completely baked. If you're not sure, check temperature with an oven thermometer.

SHORTBREAD WITH FRESH STRAWBERRIES

The shortbread provides a pleasant contrast to the acidity of fresh ripe strawberries. No sweetener or sauce is needed with the berries when served with this shortbread.

In bowl, knead until soft but still cold...	$^7/_8$	**cup**	***unsalted butter,*** chilled and diced
Knead in, in this order...	**2**	**large**	***egg yolks***
	1	**pinch**	***salt***
	$^1/_4$	**teaspoon**	***lemon zest***
	$^3/_4$	**cup**	***powdered sugar***
Knead in, 1/4 cup at a time...	$2^1/_4$	**cups**	***cake flour***

Makes a fairly stiff dough.

Roll dough in wax paper to make a 2" diameter log. Refrigerate for at least 2 hours (overnight is better). Slice log into 1/4" thick circles and place on lightly oiled baking sheet. Bake in a **preheated** 325° oven for 10-12 minutes, or until edges are just beginning to brown. Remove from oven and leave on baking sheet to cool.

Serve with fresh strawberries.

The Inn at Jackson Hole
Teton Village
733-5481

Since December 1988, connoisseurs of fine dining have found their way to The Range, a small and intimate restaurant tucked away on the second floor of The Inn at Jackson Hole in Teton Village. Its theatre style kitchen gives diners the opportunity to watch Chef Arthur Leech, owner of The Range, as he prepares their six-course dinner.

Featured in the July 1989 issue of Town and Country, and the August 1990 issue of Bon Appetit, Arthur developed his creative culinary talents as he worked under the tutelage of some fine chefs early in his career. The fixed-price dinner menus featured at The Range are his innovative interpretation of American regional cuisine, with such offerings as grilled quail under a sauce of pistachios, pork tenderloin stuffed with peaches and pecans under Southern Comfort cream, Chesapeake Bay crab cakes, and Art's signature warm salad Sausalito.

The menu and recipes Arthur shares with us here would make any dinner party a smashing success. Enjoy!

MENU FOR SIX

Herbed Chicken Pate
on Tomato Vinaigrette

Champagne Onion Soup
with Brie Cheese

Warm Salad Sausalito

Cape Cod Sorbet

Smoked Salmon
Won Ton Ravioli with
Cilantro Cream

Cappuccino Brownie Torte

Chef Arthur Leech

HERBED CHICKEN PATE ON TOMATO VINAIGRETTE

Serves 6

In food processor, puree...	1	**pound**	***chicken breasts,*** raw, boneless and skinless
Place forcemeat in bowl.			

In separate bowl, combine...	1	**cup**	***heavy cream***
	1		***egg white***
Fold into pureed chicken.			

Add and combine well...	1	**large**	***shallot,*** finely diced
	$1^1/_2$	**teaspoons**	***basil***
	$1^1/_2$	**teaspoons**	***rosemary***
	$1^1/_2$	**teaspoons**	***thyme***
			black pepper to taste

To complete this recipe, you will need...	**6-8**	**strips**	***bacon,*** uncooked

Line a terrine or loaf pan with *bacon,* firmly pack chicken forcemeat inside and top with more strips of bacon. Cover pan with foil and poke holes in it to allow steam to escape. Place terrine in a roasting pan and pour enough water in the roasting pan to come halfway up the sides of the terrine. Bake pate in this water bath in a **preheated** 325° oven for about 1 hour, until the internal temperature reaches 160°. Allow to cool to room temperature before refrigerating overnight.

To serve, place slice of pate on a pool of **Tomato Vinaigrette**.

Tomato Vinaigrette

In food processor, puree...	**4-5**	**medium**	***tomatoes,*** peeled and seeded
(You will want to have 2 cups *pureed tomato.*)			

In bowl, combine. . .	2	**cups**	***pureed tomato***
	1/2	**cup**	***olive oil***
	1/4	**cup**	***white vinegar***
	2	**teaspoons**	***basil***
			black pepper to taste

Mix well with a whip to be sure the oil emulsifies completely. Refrigerate for 1 hour.

CHAMPAGNE ONION SOUP* WITH BRIE CHEESE

Serves 6

In stockpot, combine. . .	3	**tablespoons**	***butter***
	6	**large**	***onions,*** sliced thin
Saute until onions are browned.			

Add and bring to a boil. . .	3	**quarts**	***water***
	2	**ribs**	***celery,*** cut in half
	2	**large**	***garlic cloves,*** smashed
	2	**whole**	***bay leaves***
	1	**teaspoon**	***thyme***
			black pepper to taste
Reduce to a low simmer and cook about 1-1/2 hours. Remove ribs of celery.			

To complete this recipe, you will need. . .	1/2	**cup**	***champagne,*** room temperature
	3	**ounces**	***brie***

To serve, place a slice of *brie* into each bowl and ladle hot soup over it. Lightly sprinkle about 1 tablespoon *champagne* over each bowl of soup. **It's important that the champagne be room temperature so as not to cool the soup.**

**Editor's Note: I've been lucky enough to enjoy this soup on a couple of occasions. It is one of the most delicate, light and delicious soups I've ever had!*

WARM SALAD SAUSALITO

Serves 6

The unique blend of flavors and textures make this salad a wonderful complement to any entree.

Wash, drain well and tear into bite-size pieces. . .	**2**	**heads**	***romaine***
Place in a large bowl and set aside.			

In another bowl, combine with a whip. . .	**1**	**cup**	***olive oil***
(dressing)	**1/3**	**cup**	***white vinegar***
	2 1/2	**tablespoons**	***water***
	1	**clove**	***garlic,*** minced
			black pepper to taste

In saucepan, combine and bring to a boil. . .	**8**	**ounces**	***dressing***
	1	**cup**	***pistachios***
	1	**cup**	***golden raisins***
	1/2	**cup**	***sun dried tomatoes,*** thinly sliced

To complete this recipe, you will need. . .	**1**	**large**	***red delicious apple,*** thinly sliced

Pour hot dressing over romaine and toss well. Portion salad onto serving plates and garnish each with a 'fan' of *red delicious apple* slices.

CAPE COD SORBET

Serves 6

This sorbet is a delicious and refreshing way to cleanse your palete between salad and entree course.

In saucepan, combine. . .	**12**	**ounces**	***cranberries***
	2	**cups**	***water***

Cover and simmer for about 15-20 minutes until cranberries are tender. Puree the berries along with whatever water is left.

In another saucepan, combine. . .	**2**	**cups**	***sugar***
	1	**cup**	***water***

Cover and simmer for about 5 minutes to make syrup.

To complete this recipe, you will need. . .	**1**	**cup**	***vodka***

Cool syrup in an icebath until it is cold to the touch. Combine pureed cranberries, syrup and *vodka* and pour into an ice cream freezer. Churn ice cream freezer until the sorbet becomes solid enough to stop the churning action of the freezer. Store in holding freezer until ready to serve.

SMOKED SALMON WON TON RAVIOLI WITH CILANTRO CREAM*

Serves 6

In skillet, saute...	$1^1/_2$	**teaspoons**	***vegetable oil***
	2	**large**	***shallots,*** finely diced

In bowl, combine until well blended...			***sauteed shallots***
	8	**ounces**	***smoked salmon***
	2	**tablespoons**	***heavy cream***
			black pepper to taste
Forcemeat mixture should be moist and sticky.			

To complete this recipe, you will need...	1	**package**	***won ton wrappers***
	1-2	**whole**	***eggs,*** beaten

Working with only four *won ton wrappers* at a time (keeping the rest of them covered so they won't dry out), place wrappers in front of you and put 1-1/2 teaspoons of salmon forcemeat in the center of each wrapper. Brush two edges with *egg wash* and fold the wrapper over diagonally (corner to corner), making sure the salmon forcemeat remains inside the wrapper and all air is pressed out of the ravioli while pinching the meeting edges together with your fingers. When you have made all the raviolis, allow them to set out uncovered a while to 'dry out' — this helps to seal the seams.

Before poaching the raviolis, begin making the sauce so it will be ready when the raviolis are cooked. Raviolis should be poached in water that is heated to almost boiling. Gently place raviolis into the simmering water and poach for approximately 8 minutes until wrappers become tender. Drain raviolis well before placing on plate and drape with **Cilantro Cream**.

**Editor's Note: These raviolis will melt in your mouth. Combined with the Cilantro Cream, they are truly one of the most delicious things I've ever eaten in my life!*

Cilantro Cream

In saucepan, bring a boil. . .	**1**	**cup**	***white wine***
Reduce to one third of its volume and add. . .	**3**	**cups**	***heavy cream***
Reduce until of proper consistency to coat the back of a spoon.			
Add and simmer for 1 minute. . .	**4**	**tablespoons**	***fresh cilantro,*** chopped
Remove from heat.			
Stir or swirl in until melded into sauce. . .	**3**	**ounces**	***butter,*** cold and broken into pieces

Serve immediately with ravioli.

CAPPUCCINO BROWNIE TORTE

Serves 6-8

In saucepan, melt together...	2	**ounces**	***unsweet. chocolate***
	1/3	**cup**	***shortening***

Beat in until smooth...	1	**cup**	***sugar***
	2	**large**	***eggs***

In bowl, combine...	3/4	**cup**	***flour***
	1/2	**teaspoon**	***baking powder***
	1/2	**teaspoon**	***salt***
Fold into chocolate mixture along with...	1/2	**cup**	***walnuts,*** chopped

Spread in a greased 8" springform pan and bake in a **preheated** 350° oven for 30-35 minutes. Cool completely before unmolding and spreading top with **Cappuccino Butter Cream**.

Cappuccino Butter Cream

In bowl, cream together...	1	**pound**	***butter,*** softened to room temperature
	1 1/2	**pounds**	***powdered sugar***
	1/4	**cup**	***cocoa***
	1/8	**teaspoon**	***cinnamon***
Beat until the volume of combined ingredients is increased by one third.			

Slowly blend in...	1	**large**	***egg***
	2	**tablespoons**	***rum***
	2	**tablespoons**	***espresso,*** cold

Additional powdered sugar can be added to 'dry out' the buttercream, if desired.

The Aspens
Jackson
733-1071

Opening its doors for the first time in the Fall of 1983, Stiegler's Restaurant and Bar offers authentic Austrian cuisine in an ambiance rich with the culture of that country. Peter Stiegler's philosophy of fine food, excellent service and good atmosphere in equally important proportions create a dining experience you wouldn't want to miss.

Classic Austrian cuisine, a combination of ethnic cooking from Hungary, Italy and Czechoslovakia, has not changed in 150 years. Although Peter still cooks with butter and sugar (a philosophy from his Mama, whose cooking is a large influence of Stiegler's menu), he tries to go with the times and cook a little lighter. Peter maintains that the quality of ingredients is the most important part of cooking.

Using taste more than exact recipes to create his dishes, Peter's recipes are all straight out of his head. "So, please adjust the amounts to your own tastebuds. Don't be scared! My red cabbage tastes different every time I make it!"

MENU FOR FOUR

Linguine a la Caruso

Light Cream Soup of Celery and Fennel

Tiroler Kraut Salat

Pork Medallions 'Alt Wien'

Red Cabbage Austrian Style

Heisse Liebe

Chef Peter Stiegler

LINGUINE A LA CARUSO

Serves 4

This appetizer is also wonderful as an accompaniment for a maincourse. When cooking the linguine al dente, you want it to still have a good bite.

In boiling water, cook al dente. . .	1/2	**pound**	***linguine***
Rinse with hot water and drain well.			
In skillet, heat. . .	2	**tablespoons**	***olive oil***
Add and cook 5 minutes. . .	2	**cloves**	***garlic,*** finely minced
	1	**large**	***shallot,*** finely minced
Add and cook 5 minutes more. . .	1	**large**	***tomato,*** finely diced
	1/2	**pound**	***mushrooms,*** sliced
Add and toss together. . .			***cooked linguine***
	1	**tablespoon**	***fresh basil,*** finely diced
	1	**tablespoon**	***butter,*** cold
			salt and pepper to taste

Cook a moment or two, just until linguine is hot. Serve immediately.

LIGHT CREAM SOUP OF CELERY AND FENNEL

Serves 4

In large saucepan, over medium heat, saute for 10 minutes...	1	**tablespoon**	***butter***
	1/2	**stalk**	***celery,*** finely diced
	1	**medium**	***onion,*** finely diced
Deglaze with...	1/4	**cup**	***dry sherry***
and add...	4	**cups**	***chicken broth****
	1	**teaspoon**	***fennel seeds***
Simmer for 20 minutes.			
Pour soup into food processor and blend until smooth. Put back into saucepan and add...	1/2	**cup**	***heavy cream***
			salt and pepper to taste
Bring soup up to heat.			
Ladle into serving bowls and garnish with...	2	**tablespoons**	***leeks,*** finely chopped

**Homemade is best (see recipe on page 258), or good quality canned.*

TIROLER KRAUT SALAT (WHITE CABBAGE SALAD WITH HOT BACON DRESSING)

Serves 4

In skillet, over medium high heat, combine...	1	**cup**	***bacon,*** cooked and diced
	1	**large**	***shallot,*** diced
	2	**cloves**	***garlic,*** crushed
Cook until fat is released from bacon and is hot.			

Deglaze with...	1/3	**cup**	***white wine vinegar***
and season with...	1	**teaspoon**	***caraway seeds***
			salt and pepper to taste

Pour dressing over...	1	**head**	***white cabbage,*** quartered, sliced fine julienne
Toss and serve.			

PORK MEDALLIONS 'ALT WEIN'

Serves 4

Cut into 12 medallions. . .	$1\frac{1}{2}$	**pounds**	***pork tenderloin***
Dip medallions, in this order, into. . .	$\frac{1}{2}$	**cup**	***flour***
	2	**large**	***eggs,*** beaten with 1/2 teaspoon half & half
	$1\frac{1}{2}$	**cups**	***breadcrumbs,*** spiced with salt and pepper
In large skillet, heat. . .	$\frac{1}{4}$	**cup**	***butter***
Add and saute until golden brown. . .			***pork medallions***
Remove, pat dry with paper towel, and keep warm.			
In same skillet, add and saute for 5 minutes. . .	2	**large**	***shallots,*** finely diced
	$\frac{1}{2}$	**pound**	***mushrooms,*** sliced
Deglaze with. . .	$\frac{1}{3}$	**cup**	***dry white wine***
	1	**whole**	***lemon,*** juice of (save rind for garnish)
Remove from heat and add. . .	1	**tablespoon**	***parsley,*** chopped
	1	**tablespoon**	***butter,*** cold
Swirl pan to bind sauce.			

To serve, drape pork medallions with sauce and garnish with julienne slices of lemon rind.

RED CABBAGE AUSTRIAN STYLE

Serves 4

This recipe makes more than four people will probably eat as a side dish, but leftovers are wonderful; especially when made into borscht!

In large skillet, over medium heat, saute for 7 minutes. . .	**1/4**	**cup**	***butter***
	1	**medium**	***onion,*** finely diced
	1	**large**	***apple,*** finely diced
	1	**clove**	***garlic,*** minced

Add and saute for 5 mintues. . .	**1**	**head**	***red cabbage,*** quartered, sliced fine julienne

---

Deglaze with. . .	**1**	**cup**	***red wine***
	1/3	**cup**	***red wine vinegar***
and season with. . .	**1/3**	**cup**	***sugar***
	1/4	**teaspoon**	***ground cloves***
			salt and pepper to taste

Simmer, covered, for 1 hour or until done. Cabbage should be soft with just the slightest crunch to it. Drain liquid and serve.

HEISSE LIEBE (HOT LOVE!)

Serves 4

Rich, good quality vanilla ice cream with warm homemade raspberry jam.

For this recipe, you will need. . .	1	quart	*vanilla ice cream*
	1	cup	*whipped cream*
In skillet, combine to carmelize. . .	1	tablespoon	*butter*
	1/4	cup	*sugar*
Add (and flame, if you like the show!). . .	2	tablespoons	*Framboise (or) Brandy*
Add and cook for 5 minutes. . .	1	cup	*raspberries,* fresh or frozen

Scoop *vanilla ice cream* into large-bowled wine glasses, drape with raspberry jam and top off with *whipped cream.*

A final note from Peter, "If this is a little too much to eat, reduce the size of portions or drink a good schnapps afterwards. Call me in the kitchen if you are confused about my recipes!"

Sweetwater Restaurant

Corner of King & Pearl
Jackson
733-3553

Originally a log cabin home built in 1915 by Martha and Clarence Dow, pioneers from Utah via a covered wagon, it became home to the Sweetwater Restaurant in 1976.

Over the years, the Sweetwater has seen a number of modifications and additions to the building. However, owners Steve Elzemeyer and Brad Hoch have always strived to maintain the spirit and character of the original log structure, while creating a warm and cozy environment for their patrons to enjoy while dining.

Greek specialties of moussaka and spanikopita are featured items on the Sweetwater's menu, along with a wonderful array of lamb and mesquite grilled seafood entrees. In addition to serving dinner every evening, a unique luncheon menu of original sandwiches, soups and salads is offered every day (except Sundays in the off season).

MENU FOR EIGHT

Montrechet Tart

Chilled Cranberry Soup

Tossed Green Salad
with Raspberry Poppyseed Dressing

Persian Roast Lamb

Roast Potatoes

Fresh Vegetables of Choice

Russian Cream
and Fresh Strawberries

Chef Brad Hoch

MONTRECHET TART

Serves 8

This recipe makes two tart shells (freeze one for later use) and enough filling for one tart.

In bowl, combine. . .	3	**cups**	***white flour***
	1	**teaspoon**	***salt***
	$1^1/_4$	**cups**	***crisco***
Mix with pastry knife until of cornmeal texture.			

Stir in. . .	6	**tablespoons**	***cold water***

Mix dough until you can gather it into a ball; divide the dough in half (reserving one half for a later use), and roll out 1/8" thick. Place in tart pan, trim and bake in a **preheated** 350° oven for 30 minutes. The tart shell can be made ahead to this point and refrigerated until you are ready to use it.

In bowl, gently mix together. . .	3	**ounces**	***Montrechet goat cheese,*** crumbled
	1	**tablespoon**	***olive oil***
	$^1/_4$	**teaspoon**	***thyme***
Spoon into tart shell.			

In bowl, mix together well. . .	$^3/_4$	**cup**	***half and half***
	1	**whole**	***egg***
	1	**large**	***egg yolk***
	1	**dash**	***white pepper***
Pour over cheese layer in tart shell.			

In skillet, over medium heat, carmelize until golden. . .	1	**medium**	***onion,*** thinly sliced
	1	**teaspoon**	***sugar***
Layer carmelized onions on top of tart.			

Bake in a **preheated** 350° oven for 30 minutes. Allow to sit for 15-20 minutes before serving.

CHILLED CRANBERRY SOUP

Serves 8

In saucepan, over medium heat, combine. . .	$1\frac{1}{4}$	**cups**	***sugar***
	1	**cup**	***white wine***
	$\frac{1}{2}$	**cup**	***sherry***
	1	**pound**	***fresh cranberries*** (or) 2 cans whole
Simmer until cranberries pop. Cool, then puree until smooth.			

In bowl, mix together. . .	2	**cups**	***sour cream***
	2	**cups**	***heavy cream***
	12	**ounces**	***club soda***
	1	**cup**	***orange juice***
			zest of one orange

Combine cranberry mixture with cream mixture and blend well. Chill until ready to serve.

TOSSED GREEN SALAD WITH RASPBERRY POPPYSEED DRESSING

Start with a salad of mixed greens and toppings of your choice, and dress it with our Raspberry Poppy Seed Dressing.

In food processor on high speed, combine...	2/3	**cup**	***raspberry vinegar***
	1/4	**cup**	***sugar***
	1	**small**	***onion,*** minced
	1	**large**	***egg***
	1	**tablespoon**	***dijon mustard***
	1	**tablespoon**	***poppy seeds***
	1/4	**teaspoon**	***salt***

With processor still running, slowly add...	2 1/2	**cups**	***vegetable oil***

Covered and refrigerated, dressing will keep for a week.

PERSIAN ROAST LAMB

Serves 8

Start preparing this the day before, as the lamb must marinate overnight before roasting it.

For this recipe, you will need...	**1**	**6-8 pound**	***leg of lamb,*** rolled and tied

Place *leg of lamb* in sturdy plastic bag and pour **Marinade** over it. Seal bag, place in bowl or pan and refrigerate overnight.

Take lamb out of bag (reserve marinade for basting) and place, fat side up, in a roasting pan. Bake in a **preheated** 350° oven for approximately 2-1/2 hours, or until an internal temperature of 140° for medium rare. Baste lamb with marinade and juices as it roasts. When lamb is baked to desired doneness, remove from oven and allow it to stand for 10 minutes before carving.

Potatoes can be roasted and basted with the lamb juices or separately.

Marinade

In bowl, mix together well...	**1/2**	**cup**	***chicken stock****
	1/2	**cup**	***orange juice***
	2	**tablespoons**	***lime juice***
	2	**tablespoons**	***garlic,*** minced
	2	**tablespoons**	***fresh ginger,*** grated
	1	**tablespoon**	***ground coriander***
	1/2	**teaspoon**	***cinnamon***
	1/2	**teaspoon**	***cayenne***
	1/2	**teaspoon**	***cardamon,***
	1/4	**teaspoon**	***cloves***

**Homemade is best (see recipe on page 258), or good quality canned.*

RUSSIAN CREAM WITH FRESH STRAWBERRIES

Serves 8

A simple, elegant dessert when served in wine or champagne glasses!

For this recipe, you will need. . .	**3**	**pints**	***strawberries (or) berry of choice***

Wash and hull strawberries; drain well and chill until use.

In bowl, combine. . .	**2**	**cups**	***sour cream***
	3/4	**cup**	***sugar***
	1	**teaspoon**	***vanilla extract***

Stir until sugar dissolves.

To serve, layer fruit with Russian Cream in wine or champange glass. (The Cream keeps well for 2 weeks in the refrigerator.)

MENU FOR EIGHT

Angel of Death

Cowboy Mushroom Soup

***Tossed Green Salad with
Feta, Herb and Garlic Dressing***

***Grilled Halibut
with Thai Nut Relish***

Rice Pilaf

Fresh Vegetable

Honey Custard

Chef Brad Hoch

ANGEL OF DEATH

Serves 8

Wonderfully delicious! Serve with crackers, fresh french bread or pita bread.

In mixer, blend together well. . .	1	**pound**	***cream cheese***
	1/2	**pound**	***blue cheese***
	1	**tablespoon**	***fresh garlic,*** minced
Form into heart shape or mound.			

Top with. . .	1/3	**cup**	***walnuts,*** chopped

This can be kept for 2 weeks in the refrigerator.

COWBOY MUSHROOM SOUP

Serves 8

In stockpot, over medium heat, combine. . .	2	**tablespoons**	***butter***
	1	**medium**	***green pepper,*** diced
	1	**small**	***onion,*** diced
	1 1/2	**teaspoons**	***fresh garlic,*** minced
Saute until onions are transparent.			
Add and saute for 5 minutes. . .	1	**pound**	***mushrooms,*** sliced

Add and bring to a boil. . .	2	**quarts**	***water***
	1/4	**cup**	***soy sauce***
	2	**tablespoons**	***worchestershire sauce***
	3/4	**teaspoon**	***thyme***
	3/4	**teaspoon**	***basil***
	1/2	**teaspoon**	***rosemary,*** crumbled
	1/4	**teaspoon**	***cinnamon***
Reduce to a simmer for 20 minutes.			

Increase heat to high and add. . .	**2-4**	**tablespoons**	***roux****
Stir well to break up lumps. Simmer for 5 minutes to thicken. Season with. . .			***salt and pepper to taste***

To make* ***roux**, melt 4 tablespoons butter in small pan and stir in 1/4 heaping cup of flour. Stir and cook over medium high heat until light golden brown in color.*

TOSSED GREEN SALAD WITH FETA, HERB AND GARLIC DRESSING

Start with a salad of mixed greens and toppings of your choice, and dress it with our Feta, Herb and Garlic Dressing.

In bowl, mix together well. . .	**2**	**cups**	***mayonnaise***
	1	**cup**	***cider vinegar***
	$^1/_2$	**cup**	***feta cheese,*** crumbled
	$1^1/_4$	**teaspoons**	***basil***
	$1^1/_4$	**teaspoons**	***oregano***
	$^1/_2$	**teaspoon**	***thyme***
	1	**teaspoon**	***garlic,*** minced

Whisk in slowly. . .	**1**	**cup**	***vegetable oil***

Dressing will keep for two week in refrigerator in covered jar.

GRILLED HALIBUT WITH THAI NUT RELISH

Serves 8

This Thai nut relish is delicious with any fish of your choice. Grilling the halibut on a gas or charcoal barbeque creates a wonderful taste combination with the relish; however, the fish could also be sauteed or poached.

For this recipe, you will need. . .	8	**6-8 ounce**	***halibut steaks***

Grill halibut to desired doneness (8-10 per inch of thickness is a good rule of thumb; 4 to 5 minutes per side). Place halibut on plate and top with **Thai Nut Relish.**

Thai Nut Relish

On separate baking sheets, spread. . .	1/2	**cup**	***almonds,*** slivered
	1/2	**cup**	***coconut,*** shredded
Toast in **preheated** 375° oven about 8-10 minutes, until golden brown. Cool to room temperature.			

In bowl, combine and gently toss together. . .			***toasted almonds***
			toasted coconut
	1/2	**cup**	***green onion,*** minced
	1/2	**cup**	***cilantro,*** minced
	2	**tablespoons**	***fresh garlic,*** minced
	2	**tablespoons**	***brown sugar***
	2	**tablespoons**	***soy sauce***
	4	**teaspoons**	***fresh ginger,*** grated
	4	**teaspoons**	***jalapeno pepper,*** minced

HONEY CUSTARD

Serves 8

Delicious as it is, this custard can also be flavored with 2 tablespoons of coffee or rum, or any other flavoring of your choice. Serve with whipped cream.

In large bowl, mix together...	**9**	**large**	***eggs,*** beaten
	3/4	**cup**	***honey***
	1 1/2	**teaspoons**	***vanilla extract***
	3/8	**teaspoon**	***salt***

Whisking as you pour, slowly add...	**6**	**cups**	***milk,*** scalded

Pour mixture into individual custard cups and place cups into a shallow baking pan. Fill baking pan half full with water. Bake in a **preheated** 325° for approximately 30 to 45 minutes, until knife inserted in center of a custard comes out clean.

Teton Pines Country Club
Jackson
733-1005

Nestled against the majestic Tetons, just minutes from downtown Jackson, the Teton Pines Golf Club heralds a beautiful 22,000 square-foot club house, surrounded by the 360-acre Arnold Parlmer Golf Course, the John Gardiner Tennis Center, Jack Dennis' Fly Fishing School and a 10km cross country skiing track.

As a centerpiece of this planned development, the Teton Pines clubhouse offers fine dining in an elegant atmosphere that provides magnificent views through floor to ceiling windows. For summer dining, patrons can enjoy their meals on the outdoor terrace overlooking the golf course.

Teton Pines serves lunch, dinner and Sunday brunch all year round featuring creative, regional American cuisine, offering the finest seafood, pasta, fresh baked breads and desserts. Chef Michael Hoffman has designed a menu for us which takes full advantage of the wonderful wild and fresh ingredients available in abundance in this valley we call Jackson Hole.

MENU FOR EIGHT

Forest of Wild Mushrooms

She-Crab Soup

Field of Greens Salad
with Raspberry Walnut Vinaigrette

Muscovy Duck Breast
'Weber'

Wild Rice Pilaf

Fresh Vegetable of Choice

Mocha Chocolate Cake

Chef Michael Hoffman

FOREST OF WILD MUSHROOMS

Serves 8

Using all fresh mushrooms is, of course, best when preparing this recipe. However, unless you live somewhere like Jackson Hole, where you can find and pick these wild mushroom, you will have to use dried (and rehydrated) or canned mushrooms. No matter — it will still be delicious!

Over medium high heat, in large saute pan, heat...	1	**tablespoon**	***clarified butter***
Add...	1	**tablespoon**	***shallots,*** minced
	1	**cup**	***morel mushrooms***
	1	**cup**	***chanterelle mushrooms***
	1	**cup**	***shitake mushrooms***
	1	**cup**	***button mushrooms***
Immediately follow with...	1	**tablespoon**	***fresh lemon juice***
(to fix color)	1/2	**teaspoon**	***salt***

Add...	2	**tablespoons**	***white wine***

Allow liquid to reduce by half, steaming the mushrooms.

Add...	2	**teaspoons**	***fresh parsley,*** chopped
	1	**teaspoon**	***fresh thyme leaves***
	1/2	**teaspoon**	***fresh chervil***
			black peppercorns, freshly ground to taste
Flame with...	1	**tablespoon**	***Armagnac (or) Brandy***

Add...	1 1/2	**cups**	***heavy cream***

Stir cream into mushrooms and reduce over high heat for about 5 minutes, stirring occasionally. Serve in individual gratin or rarebit dishes. Garnish with sprigs of fresh parsley if you like and serve with fresh french bread.

SHE-CRAB SOUP

Serves 8

This recipe is attributed to Martha Washington, wife of "The Father of our Country," and calls for backfin crabmeat, a delicate Maryland crab. If you can't get fresh Maryland crabs, the crabmeat is available frozen in 1-pound cans. Be sure to pick through the crabmeat for shells if using the frozen product.

In the top of a double boiler, heat until hot...	**1**	**quart**	***whole milk***
	1	**quart**	***heavy cream***
Thicken with...	**1/4-1/2**	**cup**	***roux****

Add, in this order, stirring after each addition...	**1**	**whole**	***lemon,*** grated peel and juice of
	3	**tablespoons**	***worcestershire sauce***
	1/4	**teaspoon**	***'Old Bay' seasoning***
	6	**whole**	***hard boiled eggs,*** peeled and diced
	1	**pound**	***backfin crabmeat,*** flaked
	1/4	**cup**	***dry sherry***
	2	**tablespoons**	***fresh parsley,*** chopped
			salt and pepper to taste

Stir until soup is hot and serve in warm bowls.

**To make roux, melt 4 tablespoons butter in small pan and stir in 1/4 heaping cup of flour. Stir and cook over medium high heat until light golden brown in color.*

FIELD OF GREENS SALAD WITH RASPBERRY WALNUT VINAIGRETTE

Serves 8

You're 'almost there' if you can just get your hands on edible weeds from a nearby hillside meadow! Short of that method, try the gourmet produce section at a good grocery store.

For this recipe, you will need...			***assorted lettuces*** — raddichio, American chicory, watercress, nasturnum leaves, endive, etc.
Wash and drain well, cover with a damp paper towel and refrigerate for 1 hour to crisp.			
In skillet, over medium heat, brown until golden...	1/4	**cup**	***pine nuts,*** toasted
To complete this recipe, you will need...	4	**whole**	***oranges,*** peeled and sectioned
	6	**ounces**	***feta cheese,*** crumbled

Place assorted lettuce leaves on chilled salad plates and arrange *orange sections* and *feta cheese* on top. Sprinkle with pine nuts and drizzle with **Raspberry Walnut Vinaigrette**.

Raspberry Walnut Vinaigrette

In bowl, whisk together...	1/2	**cup**	***raspberry vinegar***
	1 1/2	**teaspoons**	***fresh parsley,*** chopped
	1 1/2	**teaspoons**	***fresh thyme,*** chopped (3/4 teaspoon dried)
While continually whisking, slowly drizzle in...	1 1/2	**cups**	***walnut oil***
Season with...			***salt and pepper to taste***

MUSCOVY DUCK BREAST 'WEBER'

Serves 8

Muscovy ducks are a European variety which are less fatty and more delicate in flavor than our domestic variety. However the domestic duck, available from a good butcher, will work fine for this recipe. It's the sauce that 'makes' this dish!

For this recipe, you will need. . .			
	4	**16-20 ounce**	***duck breasts,*** boneless with skin on, halved
	2	**tablespoons**	***clarified butter***

Lightly season *duck breasts* with salt and pepper. Heat *butter* in large saute pan. Over high heat, sear duck breasts skin side down first, then turn over to sear other side. Reduce heat to low and cover; cook about 10 minutes longer to medium rare (150° internal meat temperature).

To serve, slice each breast diagonally across the grain and fan slices on a warm dinner plate. Drape generously with **Weber Sauce**.

Weber Sauce

In a thick-bottomed 2-quart saucepan, heat to carmelize. . .			
	1	**cup**	***brown sugar***
	2	**tablespoons**	***unsalted butter***

Once sugar is carmelized, add in this order, stirring to blend after each addition. . .			
	1/4	**cup**	***red wine vinegar***
	1/2	**cup**	***ruby port***
	1	**cup**	***orange juice***
	1/4	**cup**	***lemon juice***
	4	**cups**	***duck stock****
	1/4	**cup**	***Pernod Liqueur***
	3/4	**cup**	***honey***

Cook over medium high heat until carmelized sugar has dissolved.

Add. . .	2	**tablespoons**	***thyme***
	2	**tablespoons**	***ground ginger***
			salt and pepper to taste

In small bowl, combine. . .	1/2	**cup**	***vodka***
	1/4	**cup**	***cornstarch***

Using a wire whisk, incorporate cornstarch mixture into sauce while still over medium high heat. Stir until thickened.

**Homemade is best. Chicken stock can be substituted (see recipe on page 258).*

MOCHA CHOCOLATE CAKE

9" Cake

An exceptionally rich and delicious, dense cake!

In large bowl, combine and sift together thoroughly (sift 3 times). . .	3	**cups**	***flour***
	2	**cups**	***sugar***
	1	**cup**	***baker's cocoa***
	2	**teaspoons**	***baking soda***

In another bowl, using electric mixer, beat together. . .	2	**large**	***eggs***
	2	**cups**	***buttermilk***

Gradually add dry ingredients, being sure to scrape sides of bowl to thoroughly blend batter.

Add and blend well. . .	2/3	**cup**	***unsalted butter,*** melted cooled to room temp
	1	**teaspoon**	***vanilla extract***

Grease and lightly flour 2 springform cake pans and divide cake batter between them. Bake in a **preheated** 350° oven for approximately 20-25 minutes, until toothpick inserted in center comes out clean. Cool slightly in pans then unmold onto rack to cool completely.

When cakes are completely cool, spread top of one cake with **Mocha Buttercream**, top with other cake and ice completely. Garnish with mocha beans if desired.

Mocha Buttercream

In a thick bottomed 1-quart saucepan, combine...	3/4	**cup**	***heavy cream***
	1/2	**cup**	***baker's cocoa***
	1 1/4	**cup**	***powdered sugar***
	2	**tablespoons**	***instant coffee crystals***
Stir and heat until just about to scald.			
Using a wire whip, add one at a time...	3	**large**	***egg yolks***
Be sure to scrape bottom and sides of pan to cook the eggs entirely and bind the liquid. Remove from heat and **allow to cool to room temperature.**			
Add...	3/4	**pound**	***unsalted butter,*** softened to room temperature
Mix well to 'marry' butter and chocolate mixture together.			

Miscellaneous Recipes

Chicken Stock

Beef Stock

Brown Sauce

CHICKEN STOCK

Makes 2 Quarts

Canned chicken stock tends to be too salty. It doesn't really take much effort to produce your own rich chicken stock for flavoring sauces and soups.

In stockpot, combine. . .

4	**pounds**	***chicken parts,*** backs wings and necks
4	**quarts**	***water***
2	**medium**	***carrots,*** chopped
1	**large**	***onion,*** chopped
1	**rib**	***celery,*** chopped
1	**whole**	***bay leaf***
2	**teaspoons**	***thyme***
1	**teaspoon**	***black peppercorns***
3	**whole**	***cloves***
3	**sprigs**	***parsley***

Over high heat, bring to a boil. As the stock comes to a boil, foam will appear on top. Skim off the foam, reduce heat to low, and simmer for 3 to 4 hours, until liquid is reduced by half. Strain stock through a fine sieve (lined with cheesecloth, if you have it). Allow stock to cool to room temperature uncovered; then cover and refrigerate until ready to use. If you don't plan to use the stock within 2 to 3 days, freeze it.

BEEF STOCK

Makes 2 Quarts

Get beef or veal vones from your butcher – leg bones with the joints are best so there will be plenty of marrow to flavor the stock. Make sure he cuts them up into manageable-size pieces for your stockpot.

On baking sheet, place. . .	**4**	**pounds**	***beef or veal bones***

Bake in a **preheated** 375° oven for 45 minutes, until well browned.

Place browned bones in a large stockpot along with. . .	**4**	**quarts**	***water***
	2	**medium**	***onions,*** quartered
	2	**medium**	***tomatoes,*** chopped
	1	**large**	***carrot,*** coarsely chopped
	1	**rib**	***celery,*** coarsely chopped
	1	**whole**	***bay leaf***
	1	**teaspoon**	***thyme***
	1	**teaspoon**	***black peppercorns***
	6	**whole**	***cloves***
	3	**sprigs**	***parsley***
	3	**cups**	***red wine*** (optional)

Over medium heat, bring to a boil. As the stock comes to a boil, foam will appear on top. Skim off the foam, reduce heat to low, and simmer for at least 8 hours. The longer you simmer it the better it will be; simmering over a very low heat for 12 hours or overnight would be ideal. Strain stock through a fine sieve (lined with cheesecloth, if you have it). Allow stock to cool to room temperature uncovered; then cover and refrigerate until ready to use. If you don't plan to use the stock within 2 to 3 days, freeze it.

DEMI-GLACE

In large saucepan, bring to a boil 2 ***quarts beef stock***; turn heat to a low simmer and reduce stock to about 1 to 2 cups demi-glace (it has reduced to a demi-glace if it thoroughly coats the back of a spoon). Be sure to remove any scum that accumulates on the surface as it is simmering. The reduction will take several hours to be complete.

BROWN SAUCE

Makes 2 Cups

This is a simple sauce to make which will serve to enrich many other sauces. Most of the work has been done in making a good beef stock. If you don't have a good homemade stock , in a pinch you can use beef boullion (canned or from granules). But if you do, leave out the salt in this recipe.

In saucepan, heat. . .	**4**	**tablespoons**	***butter***
When butter has melted and is hot, whisk in. . .	**4**	**tablespoons**	***flour***
Stirring constantly, cook for 1 minute over medium heat.			

While constantly stirring, slowly add. . .	**2**	**cups**	***beef stock,*** heated
Continue to stir sauce until it just about comes to a boil. Remove from heat.			
Season with. . .			***salt and pepper to taste***

Leave uncovered and allow to cool to room temperature before storing, covered, in the refrigerator.

Index

E

F

G

H

I

K

L

M

T

Please send me ____ copies of ***A Taste of Jackson Hole*** at $18.95 per copy. For shipping and handling, I am enclosing $2.50 for the first book, and $1.50 for each additional book.

Cost for Cookbook(s) $______

Shipping/Handling $______

Total Amount Enclosed $_______

Make check or money order payable to: **Christine Goodman.** Send order to:

Christine Goodman
P. O. Box 3308
Jackson, Wyoming 83001

Ship to:____

Address____

City_________________________________ State_________________ Zip___________

Please send me ____ copies of ***A Taste of Jackson Hole*** at $18.95 per copy. For shipping and handling, I am enclosing $2.50 for the first book, and $1.50 for each additional book.

Cost for Cookbook(s) $______

Shipping/Handling $______

Total Amount Enclosed $_______

Make check or money order payable to: **Christine Goodman.** Send order to:

Christine Goodman
P. O. Box 3308
Jackson, Wyoming 83001

Ship to:____

Address____

City_________________________________ State_________________ Zip___________

Please send me ____ copies of ***A Taste of Jackson Hole*** at $18.95 per copy. For shipping and handling, I am enclosing $2.50 for the first book, and $1.50 for each additional book.

Cost for Cookbook(s) $______

Shipping/Handling $______

Total Amount Enclosed $_______

Make check or money order payable to: **Christine Goodman.** Send order to:

Christine Goodman
P. O. Box 3308
Jackson, Wyoming 83001

Ship to:____

Address____

City_________________________________ State_________________ Zip___________